Quantitative Methods for MBA Students, v2

Patrick R. McMullen,

Wake Forest University
School of Business

ISBN-10: 1530490200
ISBN-13: 978-1530490202

Cover Illustration by the Author:
Mandelbrot Set in Imaginary Space (Re[-0.721860, -0.721839], Im[-0.260790, -0.260778])

This book is dedicated to my Dad and the memory of my Mom.

I was lucky enough to have Mom and Dad sit through a class session of mine in 1999 when I taught at the University of Maine. It meant a lot to me to see the pride in their eyes.

Contents

Introduction

The decision to write this book was made over time and eventually out of necessity. I have seen students and their families spend much too much money for textbooks, and this in addition to skyrocketing tuition costs. The problem didn't reach a critical point with me until my children became of college age, when I experienced the high costs myself.

As such, I started on this book in September of 2015, so that students might have a good reference to help them learn introductory business statistics, while avoiding dependency on the large publishing companies and their outrageous prices.

Another reason for this book is so that there is more consistency between my lectures and the content in the book. One of the common bits of feedback from my students is that they don't like the book. I don't think the quality of the book is the problem, but the way I use the book is the problem. With this book, I will be able to better coordinate my lectures with the book, which will benefit the students. There will be a stronger relationship between the book, the lectures, and the homework assignments.

The homework problems in the book will also refer to data sets which I have created, which will also result in better coordination between lectures and assignments.

Philosophy on Quantitative Methods for MBA Students

I feel strongly that the MBA is a degree of breadth, not depth. This belief applies to the quantitative methods class as well. I am not interested in converting MBA students to become statisticians. I am interested, however, in my MBA students having an understanding of statistics to the point where they feel confident in using the tools presented, so that they may add substantial value to their organizations. I am not satisfied with students being *comfortable* in using statistics at work – I want them to be *confident* in using statistics at work.

Because of this, this book, along with my class is intended to cover the basic concepts of statistics. The esoteric nature of statistics is not of concern with this book. If the student seeks more mathematical detail of statistics, they are advised to take an advanced statistics class, an analytics class, or speak with me personally on the next steps.

On a final note regarding this matter, I also strongly emphasize the concept of parsimony in my class. That is, analyses stating what needs to be said using as few words as possible. This book was written with parsimony in mind as well – using as few words as possible to state the essentials.

Analytics Book?

I am not a fan of the term "Business Analytics." To me, it is little more than a new name for "Quantitative Methods." A trendy "buzz word," so to speak. I have looked at several "Business Analytics" books, and I see little more than a statistics book. In fact, some MBA-level Quantitative Methods books that have been around for several editions have recently been re-titled "Business Analytics" with very little change in content.

With that said, there is a field out there that deals with "analytics." This particular field concerns itself with prediction, using methodologies that have emerged in recent years. Predictions are made on things never predicted before – at least from a numerical standpoint. Analytics also concerns itself with data visualization using abstractions and new methodologies. This field of analytics continues to emerge as technology becomes more attainable.

This content of this book, however, covers classical MBA-level statistics, not analytics. The only possible exception to this is Chapter 11, which covers logistic regression.

Software

For this class, Microsoft Excel, version 2010 and later, is the software package of choice. While I do not consider Microsoft Excel the best statistics software available, it is the one software package to which essentially all students will have access. I liken Microsoft Excel's ability to perform statistics similar to a Swiss Army knife – it does a lot of things well, but no one thing exceptionally well. Microsoft Excel is flexible, and provides the tools for successful data analysis in a classroom setting.

Another software package that will be used on occasion, is JMP, a general statistical software package made by SAS. JMP goes beyond the features of Microsoft with more ease than Excel. JMP is not used as often as Microsoft Excel because of the limited availability of JMP beyond the university years. Nevertheless, JMP will be used on occasion to show some software capabilities that Excel simply cannot perform. This is especially the case when performing certain types of graphics.

Another software package that will be used on occasion is "R." R is what is known as an "open-source" software package distributed by a group of users known as the "R-project." This means that R is freely downloadable, and the users can make enhancements to the software as they see fit. The software is frequently updated, and some of the new enhancements are included with new versions, assuming the new enhancements are deemed valuable by the leadership of the R-project. R is extremely powerful software, and can handle any type of problem we encounter in this class. The only downside associated with R is that it takes a little time to become familiar with its functionality. But after the basics are learned, R becomes very useful.

Data sets are available via www.joydivisionman.com/StatBooks

Course "Prerequisites"

For this course, a basic understanding of high-school or college algebra is a must. Beyond that, some "mathematical maturity" is needed at times. In statistics, we often sum quantities and we use subscript notation to do this. It is not to appear pretentious, but it is needed to explain something as briefly as possible.

As one reads this book, particularly when trying to understand the formulae, it is important to realize that this is not "bedtime reading." It takes time to digest the concepts explained. That is why examples are provided as deemed necessary.

The other prerequisite is that it is important to have a basic understanding of Microsoft Excel. By basic understanding, it is expected that the student is able to build a formula, copy and paste, and create basic charts.

New to this Version

The major change to this version is the inclusion of a new chapter on

Logistic Regression, which delves into the R Statistical Language. This is an effort to integrate a traditional statistics class with that of the trending world of "predictive analytics."

Appendix B has been added that provides a brief tutorial on the R Statistical Language.

Also, end-of-chapter problems have been added throughout, so as to maximize the opportunity for the student to practice.

Finally, editorial changes have been made throughout, so that the readability of the book is enhanced as much as possible.

Acknowledgements

Ironically, I have the textbook publishers and university bookstores to thank for giving me the motivation to write this book. Because they form partnerships and charge the student too much money, I find an affordable textbook is now more necessary than ever.

I would like to thank my friend and colleague, Jon Pinder, for selling me on this point. Jon started doing the same thing a few years ago, with the intent of saving the students money.

I would also like to thank Mike DiCello for his help with photography, Karen Combs for her help with editing, and Vickie Whapham for her administrative help. It is also important for me to thank Kevin Bender, Pat Peacock, Carol Oliff and Chas Mansfield for their never-ending assistance in helping the students better understand the importance of the learning process.

Most importantly, I would like to thank Professor Emeritus Larry Richards of the University of Oregon. When I entered the University of Oregon in 1992, I had a real fear of statistics. While there, I had several statistics classes with Larry. Under his mentoring, I realized that I liked statistics, and that it is the most important mathematics class out there. I also learned that it would be fun to teach statistics someday. Larry's mentoring gave me the confidence to teach statistics. Larry had the ability to articulate the rigid language of statistics in a very understandable way, and I have tried to emulate him in how I explain statistics to my students.

Getting in front of a classroom full of students fearing statistics is not an easy thing to do. Larry Richards gave me the confidence to do this.

Patrick R. McMullen
Winston-Salem, North Carolina

1. Why Statistics?

Statistics is a feared entity in the business school – for both undergraduate and MBA students. I personally fit this theory given that I received a grade of "D" when I first took statistics as an undergraduate engineering student. Assuming you've not thrown your book away over that revelation, I will continue. ☺

Prior to taking statistics for the first time, I was excited about the class. The reason for this, as embarrassing as it may be, was because I thought I already had a handle on what statistics was all about. As a schoolboy, my friends and I would trade baseball cards, in our effort to have a complete collection. If I had two 1974 cards of Pete Rose, but I was lacking a 1974 Henry Aaron card, I would gladly forfeit one of my Pete Rose cards for the Henry Aaron card.

Baseball cards are rife with statistics on the player's performance throughout their careers. In 1974, Henry Aaron broke the all-time home run record, held for a long time by baseball legend Babe Ruth. When Hank Aaron accomplished this seemingly impossible feat, he forever cemented himself as a legend of the game. Table 1.1 shows selected career hitting statistics for Henry Aaron.

Career	G	AB	R	H	HR	RBI	AVG
23 Years	3,298	12,364	2,174	3,771	755	2,297	.305

Table 1.1. Selected Career Statistics of Henry Aaron

From inspection of Table 1.1, and inspection of other data sets detailing career hitting statistics, it becomes clear that Henry Aaron was unarguably one of the very best hitters in the history of the game. In fact, he has more Runs Batted In (2,297) than anyone in history, and 755 career home runs were the most ever until Barry Bonds broke the record in 2007 with 762 home runs. Unfortunately for Barry Bonds, his record will always be in doubt due to his use of performance-enhancing drugs[1]. Because of the Bonds controversy, Henry Aaron is still considered the "home-run king" by many.

Getting back to my point, this is essentially what I thought statistics was all about – studying a bunch of numbers – something similar to looking over baseball cards to learn about a player's success. I couldn't have been more wrong.

While studying over a bunch of numbers, such as numbers on a baseball card, can be considered a part of statistics, it is a very small part of statistics.

Statistics in its most general form, is learning about the population. Of course, learning about the population requires us to study the population, which is quite difficult, given the size of the population. To alleviate this problem, we collect data about the population, and this sample data is used to help us learn about the population.

While that might sound easy enough, we need to be careful on how we gather the data. It is imperative that our data be randomly sampled so as to avoid any sort of bias.

Here's an example of biased sampling. Suppose you've been given an assignment to estimate the average home price in the US. You happen to live in Brentwood, California. The easy thing to do would be to find the recent real estate transactions in your neighborhood (Brentwood), compute the average transaction price and report it as the average home price in the US.

The problem with this is pretty clear. The sample is not representative of the US population. Brentwood, California is a very affluent area, and the average home price there would be much higher than it would be for the entire US. Instead, we have to *randomly* select homes from all over the US to use for our analysis. When observations are randomly selected for our analysis, any sort of bias is avoided, and we are speaking on behalf of the population. Figure 1.1 shows a generalized version of random sampling, where the "dots" are randomly selected observations within the larger population – the boundaries of the rectangle represent the population boundaries.

---

[1] Bonds has admitted to performance-enhancing drug use, but he clarifies this by stating he never "knowingly" took performance-enhancing drugs.

Figure 1.1. Sample Data Taken from a Population

Once we have gathered our random sample from the population, we can make a proper analysis. Our intent is to learn something about our data, so that we can "tell the world" about our findings. When we "tell the world" about our findings, we are expected to use a very well-defined set of tools and semantics to articulate our findings. Quite often, we must perform a structured "test" prior to our telling the world about our findings. This formal test essentially demonstrates that proper protocol has been followed in our analyses.

In the scientific research community, any sort of substantial claim is not taken seriously unless appropriate statistical testing accompanies the claim. The business community may not be as rigid as the scientific research community, but carrying out the appropriate analyses and testing is definitely required in most situations.

Consider a company that is about to embark upon a new advertising campaign for their product. Before spending the millions of dollars to launch the campaign, they will need to "field test" the advertising campaign on focus groups, to determine if the focus groups are favorably responsive to the new advertising campaign. In order to make this determination, formal statistical analyses must be performed that convince senior management that the investment in the campaign is worthwhile.

Another example relates to the Federal Food and Drug Administration (FDA) and their possible approval of a new drug. Their job is to make certain a particular drug is effective without any dangerous side-effects. In order approve a new drug, the FDA must have *substantial statistical proof* of the drug's effectiveness without dangerous side-effects.

The formal statistical tools used to assist in such determinations and decisions are briefly described in the next section.

1.1 Tools for this Course

Given this book is for introductory purposes, a "survey" of topics are presented. They are as follows:

- **Descriptive Statistics**, which are the fundamental building block of all subsequent subjects. Here, we describe data sets in the most fundamental form possible, both numerically and graphically.
- **Probability**, which is the study of uncertainty and the likelihood of an event.
- **Random Variables**, which study the structure of certain types of data distributions.
- **Estimation**, which is how we sample from a larger population in our effort to estimate some entity and establish an interval of a specific probabilistic certainty.
- **Hypothesis Testing** is the most important topic we cover. When we make a specific claim about something, it must be accompanied by a formal test. Hypothesis testing provides us with exact structure we must use to support or refute the claim.
- **Oneway Analysis of Variance** is where we compare multiple populations and determine whether or not they are equal in value.
- **Chi-Square Testing** is where we compare a given distribution to see if it is the same as some theoretical distribution.
- **Simple Linear Regression** is another major topic in this book. In simple linear regression, we explore the possible relationship between two numerical entities. If there is a meaningful relationship, we can exploit this relationship for purposes of estimation and/or prediction of one entity given a specific value of the other entity.

- **Decision Analysis** is where we decide upon alternatives when future uncertainty is inherent. We made decisions using various strategies and we place a valuation on the degree of uncertainty.

1.2 Conclusions

It is reasonable for us to think of statistics as a "toolbox" for us to better understand our environment via a collection of data. These tools help us assess our environment. When we better understand our environment, we can improve and enhance the position of our organization, whatever that particular organization's purpose may be.

1.3 Exercises

1. Would Boston, Massachusetts be a good place to sample in order to estimate the average SAT score for all high school students? Why or why not?
2. Would the state of Ohio be a good place to sample the customer's liking to a new food product? Why or why not?
3. Why might the FDA's use of statistics be more important than other organizations use of statistics?

2. Describing Data

Statistics is all about studying data and articulating to the world our findings. Prior to our performing formal statistical tests, we need to describe the data in its most basic form. There are three basic approaches to doing this: Categorical Data Analysis, Numerical Data Analysis and the Presenting of Graphical Data.

2.1 Categorical Data Analysis

Describing categorical data is mainly a "low-tech," common sense exercise. Data of a "categorical" nature means that the data is not in numerical form, but in the form of categories. These categories are sometimes referred to as "buckets" or "bins." There is not much we can do with this data other than organizing it into a table and/or a simple chart.

For example, let's assume an apparel company is interested in targeting a demographic that frequently attends rock concerts. They are most interested in getting a handle on the color of trousers the patrons wear. As such, they hire people at the concert to tally the number of people who wear certain color jeans. They have decided on four categories: "black," "blue," "beige" and "other." In addition to the color category, they also categorize patrons by gender. After the tally, they simply present their findings in a table where each category combination is totaled, and the Gender rows are summed. The results might appear as shown in Table 2.1a.

	Black	Blue	Beige	Other	Total
Male	236	326	73	22	657
Female	158	75	42	31	306

Table 2.1a. Tally of Jeans by Gender

We can take this analysis one-step further if we present a percent breakdown of the jeans' color by gender. To do this for the men, we would divide 236 by 657 to get the percentage of black jeans, divide 326 by 657 to get the percentage of blue jeans, and so on. When we do the same for the women (dividing the frequency of each color by 306), we have the results shown in Table 2.1b.

	Black	Blue	Beige	Other	Total
Male	35.92%	49.62%	11.11%	3.35%	100%
Female	51.63%	24.51%	13.73%	10.13%	100%

Table 2.1b. Percentage of Jeans Color by Gender

Table 2.1b is probably a better way to express this data, as percentages put the tallies in a more standardized perspective as compared to raw counts.

Another way to express this data is to organize it into a column chart, where the height of each column is the percentage of jeans color, and this is done for both male and females. This particular chart was created via the "Column Chart" feature in Microsoft Excel. A pie chart is another option to show this data, where the size of each slice/wedge is the percentage of a specific color, but in recent years, the statistics community has discouraged used of pie charts because it is believed that pie charts distort perspective. As such, the column chart is shown as the preferred graphical tool for tallied data.

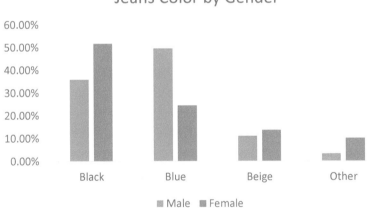

Figure 2.1. Column Chart of Jeans Color by Gender

2.2 Numerical Data Analysis

This is where our opportunity to analyze data really begins. With descriptive statistics, we can take a given set of data, calculate many statistics, and then articulate our findings in a reasonable way. There are several categories in which to describe data, but we concentrate on the most important two categories: expectation and variation.

2.2.1   Expectation

Expectation is a measure of central tendency – a singular value we can use to describe the expectation of a given data set. For example, when an instructor administers an exam, they will often state the exam average for the entire class. The instructor has summed the test scores, and divided this sum by the number of exams taken. The instructor is articulating, in essence, how the average student performed on the exam. Based upon a specific student's score then, any given student can compare their performance against the average performance. In the world of statistics, the average value of some entity is often called the **mean**.

Mathematically, we define the sample mean ($\bar{x}$) as follows, where x_i is a specific observation, referred to as the ith observation, and n refers to the number of observations in our sample. Our sample mean is as follows:

$$\bar{x} = \frac{1}{n}\sum_{i=1}^{n} x_i \qquad \text{(Eq. 2-1)}$$

The average isn't the only metric we can use to articulate central tendency. Consider a situation in which we are given an assignment to estimate the expected home value in King County, Washington. We decide to randomly sample 10 houses in the area for our estimation. It turns out that one of the ten houses we use is the home of Microsoft founder Bill Gates. Mr. Gates' home is worth several million dollars – much higher than the other home values in our collection of data. This will severely bias our average – it would inflate our average and misrepresent the expected home value in King County, Washington. Instead of calculating the average, we can sort our data from low to high (or high to low) and selected the "middle value" for an odd number of observations, or average the "middle two" values for an even number of observations. This value is called the **median**, and is often used on socioeconomic data to eliminate any biases associated with extreme values.

Another measure of central tendency, although perhaps not as important as the mean and standard deviation is the **mode** – the most frequently observed value in a collection of data. Sometimes, depending on the nature of the data, there will not be a mode. Sometimes, there may be multiple modes. For example, where a data set contains two unique modes, the data can be referred to as "bi-model."

In Microsoft Excel, the built-in functions for the measures of central tendency are shown in Table 2.2. In this context, and throughout the book, the term "*data range*" refers to the actual data set being referred to while in Excel.

Statistic	Excel Formula
Mean	=average(*data range*)
Median	=median(*data range*)
Model	=mode(*data range*)

Table 2.2. Excel Formulae for Central Tendency

2.2.2 Variation

Variation is an underappreciated and overlooked part of descriptive statistics, but a very important one. In fact, it is just as important as the measures of central tendency. The reason it is so underappreciated is because it is not terribly well understood. In fact, when I didn't do well the first time I took statistics, my misunderstanding of variation was a large reason why.

Variation measures dispersion of the data set. That is the most general form of variation, which we can capture that value by the **range** (*Range*), which is the difference between the minimum observed value (x_{min}) and the maximum observed value (x_{max}). Mathematically, this is as follows:

$$Range = x_{max} - x_{min} \qquad \text{(Eq. 2-2)}$$

While this version of dispersion is simple to calculate, it is naïve because it does not account for dispersion of the observations with respect to the mean. The value that best captures dispersion about the mean is the **sample standard deviation**, s. At first glance, the mathematics of this equation may seem intimidating, but with some explanation, it should become more understandable. The sample standard deviation is as following:

$$s = \sqrt{\frac{\sum_{i=1}^{n}(x_i - \bar{x})^2}{n - 1}}$$

(Eq. 2-3)

This calculation calculates the difference between each observation and the sample mean. This difference is squared. It is squared for two reasons: the first reason is to eliminate a negative number in the calculation, as any number squared is a positive number; the second reason is to amplify big differences between the observed value and the sample mean. These squared differences are then summed, which accounts for the numerator of the equation. The numerator is then divided by (n - 1). The division by n is to put the calculated quantity into the same units as the observed data – similar to dividing by n when a sample mean is calculated. The value of "1" is subtracted from n to account for the fact that we have limited data – sample information instead of population data. The subtraction of "1" from n adjusts the sample standard deviation upward, "inflating" our estimate of the standard deviation, as compared to the standard deviation of the population. Fortunately, this formula is rarely used in practice, as Excel and other software packages easily make the calculation.

Another formula, used to calculate the sample variance is the squared value of the sample standard deviation, and is shown here:

$$s^2 = \frac{\sum_{i=1}^{n}(x_i - \bar{x})^2}{n - 1}$$

(Eq. 2-4)

The only difference between the two is that the sample standard deviation is the square root of the sample variance, and is more commonly used, because its value is in the same units as the observed value.

In Excel, the formulae for range, standard deviation and sample variance are as follows:

Statistic	Excel Formula
Range	=max(*data range*) − min(*data range*)
Sample Standard Deviation	=stdev(*data range*)
Sample Variance	=var(*data range*)

Table 2.3. Excel Formulae for Variation

Now that we have the tools to describe central tendency and variation, a brief time is spent discussing the distribution of the data set.

2.2.3   Distribution

Many observations comprise a data set. Each individual observation has a "position" in the data set, so to speak. When the data is sorted, we can "see" where a certain observation fits in with the rest of the data. Excel, JMP and other software packages tell provide us with the position of an observation in a data set without our having to sort or otherwise manipulate the data. In particular, we can calculate **percentiles** and **quantiles** associated with a data set.

The percentile of an observation in a data set is its relative position to other observations in that same data set. You should be familiar with this concept. If/when you took the GMAT, SAT or ACT exam, you were given a numerical score which probably didn't mean much to you, because you have no basis for comparison. But you were also presented with percentile data, which told you how you did when compared to the performance of *all* test-takers. For example, if your percentile score was 75, you scored better than 75% of all test-takers.

The percentile of a data set basically breaks down the data into 100 pieces, or percentiles. The quartile of a data set basically breaks down the data into four pieces. The first quartile is tantamount to the 25th percentile, the second quartile is tantamount to the 50th percentile (which we also refer to as the median), and the third quartile is tantamount to the 75th percentile. The fourth quartile, which we never use, is essentially the maximum observed value.

In Excel, these values are easily computed using the *percentile* and *quartile* functions.

Statistic	Excel Formula
Percentile	=percentile(*data range, value*)
Quartile	=quartile(*data range, quartile value*)

Table 2.4. Excel Formulae for Percentiles and Quartiles

For example, if we have a data set called "X" with several observations, the function "=percentile(X, 0.63)" will return the value in the data set associated with the 63rd percentile. If we use the function "=quartile(X, 3)," the function will return the value in the data set associated with the 3rd quartile (or 75th percentile). Note that for the percentile function, our value must be between 0 and 1. The 0th percentile is the minimum value in the data set, while the 100th percentile is the maximum value in the data set. For quartile values, our quartile value must be either 0, 1, 2, 3 or 4. The 0th quartile is the minimum value in the data set, while the 4th quartile is the maximum value in the data set. It should be noted, however, that the 0th quartile and the 4th quartile are of no practical value, as they respectively imply the minimum and maximum values.

It should be noted that the functions shown in Table 2.4 assume that we intend for the highest value possible to occur – as in a test score, for example. If we seek the lowest score possible, we simply replace "=percentile(*data range, value*)" with "1 – percentile(*data range, value*)." For quartiles, we simply switch the values for the first and third quartiles.

We have restricted our coverage of "distribution" to percentiles and quartiles. There are other measures of distribution, such as **skewness** and **kurtosis** which are beyond the scope of this book. In the next section, we will continue to discuss the distribution of a data set, but in a more conceptual manner.

2.3 Presenting Graphical Data

A picture is worth a thousand words. Statistics is no exception to that adage. Today's computer and software resources have greatly enhanced our ability to visualize data. Thirty years ago, our ability to visualize data was essentially constrained to a handheld calculator, pencil and paper. Bad memories. ☹

While there are countless tools to present data in a graphical format, our pursuit of presenting graphical data will be confined to the **histogram** and the **boxplot**.

2.3.1 Histogram

Without question, the histogram is the most common way to graphically present **univariate** (single variable) data. When we have a collection of data, it is wise to organize the data based on similarity – we did this in Section 2.1, where we categorized the jeans that the concert-goers wore by gender and by the color of jeans. Now that we are dealing with numerical data, similarity can be categorized much easier. Numbers that are "similar" can be numbers that are close in value. In a histogram, we have two axes: the horizontal axis (often referred to as the "x-axis") is a listing of numerical outcomes in ascending order. The vertical axis (often referred to as the "y-axis") is the **frequency** (how often) each outcome was observed. A histogram is sometimes referred to a frequency chart.

Outcome is a subjective assessment and some thought is required as to how to manage outcomes. For example, if I were give an exam to my students, the minimum score might be 70 while the maximum score might be 100. The outcomes would be easy to itemize: 70, 71, 72, ..., 100. This, however, is only one way to structure outcomes. As critic of this approach might think there is too much detail in these outcomes, particularly if the class is small. They might suggest fewer outcomes, perhaps only even-numbered scores: 70, 72, 74, ..., 100. Under this revised scenario, odd-numbered scores would be placed into the lower category or higher category – it really doesn't matter, provided all odd-numbered scores are treated the same.

The point of the above is to suggest that some thought should go into how outcomes are organized. One rule of thumb is that a good number of categories to use when deciding how many outcomes to have is a function of the number of observations in the data set, which we will call "n." This particular rule of thumb suggests that $\sqrt{n}$ is a good number of categories to use. I agree with this rule of thumb, but I generalize it even more – for large data sets (~ 500 observations), I like to use about 25 categories. For larger data sets ($\geq$ 1000 observations), I like to use about 30 or so categories.

Fortunately, most fully-dedicated statistical software packages like JMP and R automatically choose how many categories to use, but this can be controlled by the user. For Excel, the number of categories must be pre-determined.

Let's build a histogram with some data. Let's assume that it was "Las Vegas Night" at the business school. Staff, students and faculty played a few casino games for small amounts of money, and the "money lost" by the players went to a charitable cause. There were 120 participants, and their "winnings" are shown below in Table 2.5. Negative winnings are, of course, losses and are preceded by a "minus sign."

From close inspection of Table 2.5, the worst performance was a loss of $10.00, and the best performance was a gain of $2.00, making for a range of -10 to 2. It seems reasonable to have categories starting at -$10 and ending with $2, and having them in $1 increments, for a total of 13 categories. Incidentally, 13 total categories is reasonably close to the rule of thumb number of categories of $\sqrt{n}$.

-3.75	-6.00	-8.50	-2.75	-0.50	-5.50	-6.00	-4.75	-6.50	-5.25
-7.50	-6.75	-4.75	-3.25	-5.75	-1.00	-1.00	-5.50	-5.75	-3.75
-1.75	0.75	-0.75	-0.50	-2.00	1.75	-2.75	1.75	-5.75	-2.50
-2.25	-1.25	-3.25	-5.75	-5.25	-3.00	-6.25	-5.25	-4.75	-7.75
-3.25	-2.25	-2.00	-4.50	-3.00	-8.25	-4.00	0.00	0.75	-1.50
-6.75	-2.25	-4.25	-6.25	-7.25	-2.50	1.25	-1.75	-3.00	-4.75
-9.50	-4.50	-4.25	-1.50	-4.25	-8.50	-3.00	-2.25	-3.00	-5.50
-5.00	-3.75	-4.25	-2.25	-3.75	-1.25	-6.50	-5.50	-6.50	-5.25
-0.75	-3.00	-4.50	-1.75	-3.00	-4.50	-2.50	-2.25	-4.50	-6.00
-3.50	-6.00	-2.25	-6.00	-3.50	-6.00	-0.75	-2.75	-1.50	-1.50
-3.25	-8.50	-2.75	-4.75	-6.25	-1.00	0.25	-5.00	-3.50	-10.00
-7.25	-2.75	-1.75	-2.00	-2.25	-3.25	2.00	-3.50	-0.50	-8.25

Table 2.5. Winnings from Las Vegas Night

The histogram can be generated in Excel via Data | Data Analysis | Histogram. From there, you are asked for two groups of data: the first is the "Input Data," which is the 120 actual observations; the second is the "Bin Range," which is an ordered list of categories, which, in this case, is -$10, -$9, ..., $1, $2. Excel then returns the frequencies of each categorized outcome, which is shown in Table 2.6.

Outcome Category	Frequency	Relative Frequency
-$10	1	0.83%
-$9	1	0.83%
-$8	5	4.17%
-$7	4	3.33%
-$6	14	11.67%
-$5	14	11.67%
-$4	15	12.50%
-$3	20	16.67%
-$2	19	15.83%
-$1	13	10.83%
$0	7	5.83%
$1	3	2.50%
$2	4	3.33%

Table 2.6. Frequencies of "Winnings" from Las Vegas Night

A histogram using the frequency data from Table 2.6 is shown in Figure 2.2.

Figure 2.2. Histogram of Las Vegas Night

You will notice from Figure 2.2 that this histogram is nothing more than a column chart, with the horizontal axis being the ordered categories, and the vertical axis being the frequencies.

It should also be noticed that the rightmost column of Table 2.6 is entitled "**Relative Frequency**." For each outcome category, we can convert the frequencies to relative frequencies by dividing the frequency value by the total number of observations, which is 120 in this case. For example, the -$4 category has a frequency of 15. The relative frequency of this category is 12.50% (15/120). It would be of no particular benefit to show a histogram of the relative frequencies, because the column heights would be exactly proportion to the column heights of the frequency histogram in Figure 2.2. The only difference between a frequency and a relative frequency is that the frequencies will sum to the number of observations, while the sum of the relative frequencies will sum to 1.

In terms of the histogram itself, we see that losses of about $3 is the most frequent outcome. Without getting into descriptive statistics at present, we can reasonably conclude some form of central tendency of an approximate $3 loss. This will be discussed further in the next section.

Figure 2.3 shows a very nice example of a histogram. It illustrates income distribution in 2011. The horizontal axis shows annual income categories in $5,000, where the vertical axis shows the relative frequencies of these outcomes.

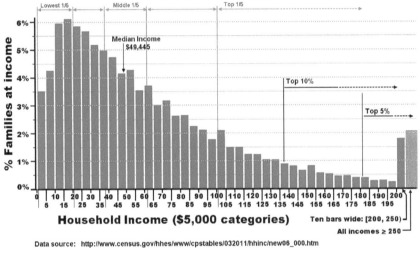

Data source: http://www.census.gov/hhes/www/cpstables/032011/hhinc/new06_000.htm

Figure 2.3. Histogram of Income Distribution

The histogram has a few properties worth noting. First, we might notice that most outcomes reside on the left – lower incomes, with a decreasing frequency of higher incomes, until we get to the $200K and more category. The median, a measure of central tendency, resides in the "hump," while there is a dominant tail to the right. We use the term "**skewed right**" to describe this type of distribution – the tail is to the right of the "hump." A distribution that is "**skewed left**" is where the dominant tail is to the left of the "hump." If a distribution is not skewed either way, we call the distribution **symmetric**.

2.3.2   Box Plot

As stated earlier, the histogram is the most important tool we have to present descriptive statistical data in graphical form. The **box plot**, however, does provide us with additional insight regarding the distribution. The box plot is more of an abstraction than the histogram and requires some explanation. The box plot shows us the first quartile, the second quartile (median) and the third quartile as vertical lines composing a box. The first quartile is the left edge of the box, while the third quartile is the right edge of the box. The median is somewhere between these two edges. We then compute "thresholds" or "fences" to determine "**outliers**." There is a lower threshold and an upper threshold. Each of these are 1.5 times the interquartile range $(Q_3 - Q_1)$. Mathematically, these thresholds are determined as follows:

$$\text{Lower Threshold} = Q_1 - 1.5*(Q_3 - Q_1) \qquad \text{(Eq. 2-5)}$$

$$\text{Upper Threshold} = Q_3 + 1.5*(Q_3 - Q_1) \qquad \text{(Eq. 2-6)}$$

Any values that are below the lower threshold or above the upper threshold are considered outliers – extreme observations. "Whiskers" are then drawn in. The lower whisker is drawn from the first quartile to correspond to the smallest value in the data set above the lower threshold. Similarly, the upper whisker is drawn from the third quartile to the highest value in the data set below the upper threshold. Values in the data set outside of these two thresholds are considered outliers and are highlighted as such. It is possible for a box plot *not* to have outliers. The figure below shows a generalized box plot in the context as described.

It is important to note that various books and software packages give slightly different treatments to boxplots, particularly with respect to how whiskers and outliers are determined. What is consistent, however, for all box plots, is that the first and third quartiles, along with the median are always given the same treatment.

2.4 Putting it All Together

This section is concerned with making a proper statistical reporting given a data set, and using our descriptive statistical tools and our graphical tools. For illustrative purposes, we will use our Las Vegas Night data set, and JMP to assist with the analysis.

Once the JMP software is started, we can import an Excel data set. From there, asking JMP to make the statistical analyses is very easy. While in JMP, we select "Analyze," then "Distribution." From there, we select our variable for the "Y, Columns" box and click "Go." At this point, JMP returns an immense amount of output, most of which we do not need. Once we are in output mode, we can eliminate which output we do not wish to see, and focus on what we do want to see, by unchecking various output options – this (selecting which output to see) is something that requires experimentation. The figure below is a JMP screen capture of our Las Vegas Night analyses – all of these outputs are standard with JMP.

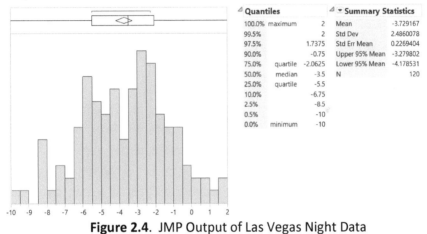

Figure 2.4. JMP Output of Las Vegas Night Data

The first thing I notice is that the average winnings are -$3.73. In other words, I can expect to lose $3.73, which is quite similar to the median value of -$3.5. I also notice a standard deviation of $2.49, and first and third quartiles of -$5.5 and -$2.06. The next thing I do is examine the histogram, which is essentially the same as Figure 2.2. Here, the x-axis of the histogram was manipulated to see increments of $1.

A very nice feature of JMP is that it places a box plot on top of the histogram – this permits us to the see the relationship between the two graphical tools, providing us a better perspective of the data set. JMP offers two box plot features not shown via other software packages. In the box plot, you will notice a diamond-shaped figure. The part of the diamond where it is at its maximum height is the mean value of the data set. The width of the diamond shows us a 95% confidence interval, which we will talk about in Chapter 5. The red bracket just above the box plot is referred to as the "shortest half," which displays the highest-density collection of 50% of the observations in the data set.

Earlier in my teaching career, I never covered the box plot. I restricted my conversation to the histogram when covering graphical approaches to descriptive statistics. In recent years, however, I have come to embrace the box plot. While it is definitely less concrete than the histogram, it does provide us with a tremendous amount of information in a particularly simple way. As such, I now consider it an enhancement to the histogram.

2.5 Conclusions

None of the concepts in this chapter are particularly difficult – I state this from both a mathematical *and* conceptual perspective. Despite the relative simplicity of this subject matter, none of it should be discounted as unimportant. Descriptive statistics is perhaps the most important subject covered in this book. When we talk about a data set, we should ALWAYS summarize the data in numerical/statistical form, and use graphical support, as many people in business, particularly those without a numerical background, place more value on the pictures than they do the numbers.

2.6 Exercises

For problems 1 – 6, use the "ExamScoresData" data set. For problems 7 – 12, use the "WireGaugeData" data set.

The "ExamScoresData" data set records scores for two exams taken by a group of students. The students took Exam 1 prior to their taking Exam 2.

1. Using Excel, please address the following:
    a. The mean values for Exam 1 and Exam 2.
    b. The median values for Exam 1 and Exam 2.
    c. The standard deviation values for Exam 1 and Exam 2.
    d. The lowest score of the two exams, and the highest score of the two exams.
2. Using Microsoft Excel, create a combined histogram for each exam using a bin range in increments of 2 exam points.

3. Using Microsoft Excel, created a combined histogram for each exam using a bin range in increments of 1 exam point.
4. Using your histogram from Problem 3, distinguish the performance between Exam 1 and Exam 2.
5. Do the histograms provide any help in determining how the data is distributed. Comment on the data distributions.
6. Using JMP, construct box plots for Exams 1 and 2. Do your findings support your answer in Problem 4?

For the "WireGaugeData" data set, data was taken from two shifts in a factory where the diameter of 22-gauge wire was measured. It is intended for the wire to have a diameter of 0.64mm.

Using Excel, please compute the following:

7. The mean wire diameter for Shifts 1 and 2.
8. The median wire diameter for Shifts 1 and 2.
9. The standard deviation of the wire diameter for Shifts 1 and 2.
10. Between the two shifts, what is the smallest wire diameter, and what is the largest wire diameter?
11. Using Excel, create a combined histogram using 30 bins, positioned between the minimum and maximum wire diameters.
12. Using JMP, create a box plot for each shift.

13. Using your findings from Problems 7 and 9, talk about the distribution for each shift.
14. Which shift does a better job in achieving the targeted diameter of 0.64mm?
15. Which shift is more consistent in terms of wire diameter?

3 Probability

We encounter probability every day in our lives. We watch the news on TV and learn that there will be a slight chance of rain tomorrow afternoon. Sometimes, a probability of rain will even be given explicitly. If we watch news about politics, we will even see political pundits estimating probabilities of candidates being elected to various forms of political office.

In the specific sense, probability is the likelihood of some event occurring. In the general sense, probability is the study of uncertainty. While this chapter might focus on studying the likelihood of some event occurring, the remainder of the book is certainly more focused on studying uncertainty, as this concept is very important when we turn to hypothesis testing in the latter chapters of this book.

3.1 Basic Probability

This section addresses the most common-sense aspects of probability. Let us begin by referring to some event as "A." The probability of event A occurring is the ratio of how many times A can occur to all trials in the experiment. A simple example is where we are interested in determining the probability of drawing a "6" from a standard deck of 52 cards. We know that there are four different possibilities of "6" in a standard deck of cards (clubs, diamonds, hearts, and spades). There are, then, four cards of "6" in a deck of cards, making our probability of drawing a "6" four chances in 52, or 4/52, which is 7.69%.

The probability of drawing a "6 of clubs" is different than the above probability. The deck of cards has only one card that fits this description. Because of this, our chances of drawing a "6 of clubs" from a standard deck of cards is 1/52, which is 1.92%.

The probability rules in the next section provide some tools that assist us in understanding slightly more complex probabilistic issues.

3.2 Probability Rules

Prior to presenting the actual rules, there are a few terms which need to be defined, so that the probability rules are more clearly understood.

As stated previously, $P(A)$ is the notation we use to describe the probability of event A occurring. Related to that is the notation $P(\bar{A})$, which we refer to as the probability of event A not occurring, or "the probability of **'A-compliment.'"**

Another item of business which must be covered involves **mutually exclusive events** and **independent events**. Mutually exclusive events are events that cannot happen at the same time – events where only one specific outcome can occur. An example of a mutually exclusive event is where we sample from a larger population to study something. Our subjects can only be male or female – never both. As such, the gender of an individual can be thought of as a mutually exclusive event. Another example is a student's application to a university. There are three possible outcomes: acceptance, rejection, or "wait-list." When a student receives their decision letter from a university, the outcome will only be ONE of three possible outcomes, never any combination of the possible outcomes.

Independent events *can* happen at the same time – these events are independent of other events. Let's assume that the New York Yankees are playing the Boston Red Sox tonight. Meanwhile, the Pittsburgh Pirates are playing the Cincinnati Reds. It is possible that both the Yankees and the Pirates win because they are not playing each other – they have other opponents. The Yankees / Red Sox game and the Pirates / Reds games are independent of each other.

To understand the probability rules shown below, it is of great importance to understand the difference between mutually exclusive events and independent events.

3.3.1   Probability Rule 1

The probability of some event will always be between zero and one. A probability can never be less than zero, nor can it be greater than one. Mathematically, this is as follows:

$$0 \le P(A) \le 1 \qquad \text{(Eq. 3-1)}$$

This rule applies to both mutually exclusive and independent events.

3.3.2   Probability Rule 2

For mutually exclusive events, only one of the possible events can occur. If there are four possible events (A, B, C and D), one of them must occur. Mathematically, we can state this as follows:

$$P(A) + P(B) + P(C) + P(D) = 1 \qquad \text{(Eq. 3-2)}$$

3.3.3   Probability Rule 3

If event A does not occur, its complement $\bar{A}$ must occur. Mathematically, this means two things:

$$P(A) + P(\bar{A}) = 1 \qquad \text{(Eq. 3-3)}$$

$$P(\bar{A}) = 1 - P(A) \qquad \text{(Eq. 3-4)}$$

This rule applies to both mutually exclusive and independent events.

3.3.4   Probability Rule 4

For mutually exclusive events, the probability of event A or event B occurring is the sum of the probabilities. Mathematically, this can be said as follows:

$$P(A \text{ or } B) = P(A) + P(B) \qquad \text{(Eq. 3-5)}$$

It should also be stated that another way of stating P(A or B) is to say P(A$\cup$B), which implies the "**union**" of A and B. As an example, there is 10% probability that I will have pizza for dinner tonight, and a 15% probability that I will have pasta for dinner. Therefore, there is a 25% probability (10% + 15%) probability that I will have either pizza or pasta for dinner tonight.

3.3.5   Probability Rule 5

For independent events, we can calculate the probability of both events A and B happening via the following relationship:

$$P(A \text{ and } B) = P(A) * P(B) \qquad \text{(Eq. 3-6)}$$

We can also state P(A and B) as P(A $\cap$ B), which we call the "intersection" of events A and B.

There is a probabilistic tool known as a "**Venn Diagram**," which can help us visualize these types of things. For the independent events A and B, the

Venn Diagram provides visual support for the above equation. For example, let us assume that there is a 60% chance the Yankees will beat the Red Sox, and there is a 55% chance that the Pirates will beat the Reds. The probability of both the Yankees and Pirates winning is, therefore, (0.60)(0.55) = 0.33, or 33%. For this calculation, we are essentially calculating the section of the circles that overlap in Figure 3.1.

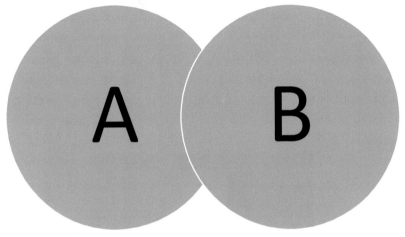

Figure 3.1. Venn Diagram of Events A and B

3.3.6   Probability Rule 6

For independent events, the probability of either events A or B occurring is as follows:

$$P(A \text{ or } B) = P(A) + P(B) - (P(A) * P(B)) \qquad \text{(Eq. 3-7)}$$

Again, the notation P(A or B) can also be shown as P(A $\cup$ B). To continue with our example, the probability of either the Yankees or Pirates winning their game is (0.60 + 0.55 − (0.60 * 0.55)), which is 0.82, or 82%.

3.3 Contingency Tables

There are times when we have the opportunity to study mutually exclusive events where there are two factors involved, as opposed to a single factor as described above. If we have one factor with *a* possible mutually exclusive outcomes and another factor with *b* possible mutually exclusive outcomes, we have a **contingency table** with *a* rows and *b* columns, and *a*b* table entries. For each cell in the table, we are given the number of outcomes that are associated with each unique combination of the two factors. This contingency table provides with probabilistic information regarding each factor and all combinations of factor levels.

Consider an example of the US House of Representatives voting on a house resolution – voting on whether or not a bill should become a law. Two factors of interest here are first, the party affiliation – this factor has two levels: Republican and Democrat.   The second factor is how the representative voted on the resolution. This factor also has two levels: Yes and No. Because each factor has two levels, we have four combinations. For our example, we study House Resolution 1599, which was brought to the House of Representatives on July 23, 2015. The name of the resolution is the "Safe and Accurate Food Labeling Act." The contingency table of this vote is as follows:

	Yes	No	Total
Republican	230	12	242
Democrat	45	138	183
Total	275	150	425

Table 3.1. House Vote on HR 1599

The first order of business is to determine whether or not the bill passed the house. It did, by a 275 – 150 margin. I look at the column total for "Yes" and I compare it to the column total for "No" to make this determination. I also notice that 242 Republicans voted, while 183 Democrats voted. I make this determination by looking at the row totals. Finally, I arrive at a value of 425 total votes – this value can be determined by adding the row totals *or* the column totals. This value can also be determined by adding the values of the four factor-level combinations (230 + 12 + 45 + 138). 425 is the total number of observations, which we can refer to as *n*.

If we were to divide all numbers in our contingency table by *n*, we would get probabilities, which standardize our frequency data. By doing this, we are essentially building a table of relative frequencies. Table 3.2 shows the results of this.

	Yes	No	Total
Republican	54.12%	2.82%	56.94%
Democrat	10.59%	32.47%	43.06%
Total	64.71%	35.29%	100%

Table 3.2. Relative Frequencies of HR 1599

From Table 3.2, we see that 56.94% of the votes were cast by Republicans, and 43.06% of the votes were cast by Democrats. We also see that 64.71% of the vote was "Yes," while 35.29% of the vote was "No." The political party votes will sum to 100%, while the "Yes" vs "No" votes will also sum to 100%. These values are referred to as "**marginal probabilities**" because they are on the "margins," or edges of the contingency table. In essence, they tell us how each of our factors are divided. We can state these marginal probabilities in mathematical notation as well. For example, we can say the following about Democrats: P(Democrat) = 43.06%.

Figure 3.2 also provides with "**joint probabilities**," values showing us the probability of specific combinations of our factors occurring. For example, 2.82% of Republicans voted No on HR 1599. Note that both factors are considered for this joint probability. We can state this mathematically via the following: P(Repubican and No) = 0.0282. The notation P(Repubican $\cap$ No) is also reasonable notation.

The final topic we discuss relative to contingency tables is the concept of **conditional probability**. The conditional probability of an event occurring is the probability of that event occurring given that some other event has occurred. Mathematically, this is as follows:

$$P(A \mid B) = P(A \cap B) / P(B) \qquad \text{(Eq. 3-8)}$$

In this particular notation, the "|" means "given," so we are implying the probability of A given B. Said as simply as possible, we'd like to find the probability of even A occurring knowing that event B has already occurred.

For example, we can calculate the probability of a voter voting "No" with the prior knowledge that they are a democrat. In the context of this example, we determine this as follows:

$$P(\text{No} \mid \text{Democrat}) = P(\text{No} \cap \text{Democrat}) / P(\text{Democrat}) \quad \text{(Eq. 3-9)}$$

The calculation for this would be 0.3247 / 0.4306 = 0.7541. In other words, there is a 75.41% chance that a representative will vote "No" provided they are a Democrat.

If someone votes "Yes," what is the probability they are a Republican? We can address this question as follows:

$$P(\text{Republican} \mid \text{Yes}) = P(\text{Yes} \cap \text{Republican}) / P(\text{Yes}) \quad \text{(Eq. 3-10)}$$

For this question, we employ 0.5412 / 0.6471, which results in 0.8364. In other words, given that a representative votes "Yes," the probability of them being Republican is 83.64%.

Contingency Tables are a valuable exercise in better understanding probability. We often find useful information in studying outcomes when two variables of the mutually exclusive variety are present. We conclude this chapter by focusing on the number of possible outcomes via a brief introduction to "counting."

3.4 Basic Counting

As defined at the beginning of this chapter, the probability of a specific event occurring is the number of possible successes divided by the number of possible outcomes. Quite often, determining the number of possible outcomes is a bit tricky, and quite often, this number is shockingly large. With a few basic mindsets, we can discipline ourselves to finding the number of outcomes by understanding what tools need to be used to make the appropriate calculation. There are three basic approaches we will take: the product rule, understanding combinations, and understanding permutations. This topic is a branch of probability often referred to as **combinatorics**, which is, in my opinion covered too infrequently in our statistics books.

3.4.1 The Product Rule

Often we have a number of factors, each having a specific number of levels. To determine the number of possible outcomes, we can employ the product rule. In its simplest form and from a mathematical perspective, the product rules is as follows

$$\text{Outcomes} = \prod_{i=1}^{m} n_i, \qquad \text{(Eq. 3-11)}$$

Where n_i is the number of levels for factor level i, and the upper case "pi" symbol (Π) means multiply, similar to how the upper "sigma" sign (Σ) means to sum.

As an example, let's consider pizza options. There are four factors: crust, cheese, topping and size. Table 3.3 details these factors. For this example, it is assumed that for each factor, exactly one level is permitted.

Factor	Number of Levels	Levels
Crust	4	Thin, Thick, Deep Dish, Pan
Cheese	4	Mozzarella, Provalone, Romano, Gouda
Topping	30	Anchovy, Bell Pepper, ..., Pinapple
Size	4	Individual, Medium, Large, Family

Table 3.3. Pizza Options

The number of unique pizza combinations is simply determined by the product of the number of levels for all factors: (4)*(4)*(30)*(4) = 1,920. This example shows that there are 1,920 outcomes. Of course, some of these outcomes are more likely than others in reality, but that fact is beyond the scope of our present conversation.

3.4.2 Combinations

In the previous paragraph, the word "combination" is used somewhat informally. In this section, we use the word "combination" more formally. Given we have n unique items in a set, and we wish to select a subset of size r from the set, the number of unique combinations we have is often referred to as "n choose r." Another way to state this is C(n, r) or $_nC_r$. For the remainder of this book, the C(n, r) notation will be used. With these definitions now known, the number of combinations can be determined as follows:

$$\text{Combinations} = C(n, r) = \frac{n!}{r!(n-r)!} \qquad \text{(Eq. 3-12)}$$

Here, $n!$ means "n-factorial," which is defined as follows:

$$n! = n * (n - 1) * (n - 2)...(2) * (1) \qquad \text{(Eq. 3-13)}$$

The factorial concept will be better detailed in the next section.

As an example of combinations, let's look at the following example. I have a collection of ten books, and I'm about to go on a long trip. I only have room for three books. How many book combinations are there? For this question, we have a set of ten items ($n = 10$) and we are seeking a subset of size three ($r = 3$). Using our combinations formation from Eq. 3-12, we can determine that there are 120 possible book combinations.

3.4.3   Permutations

Combinations are insensitive to ordering. For our book example above, we calculated how many possible combinations there are of size three from ten total items. These 120 combinations are insensitive to any sort of order. For example, books "A," "B" and "C" are the same as books "C," "A," and "B." For permutations, however, we *are* sensitive to ordering. A permutation is a unique ordering from a set of n items, when we take a subset of r items. Notation for permutations is similar to that of combinations – we use $_nP_r$ and $P(n, r)$ to mean the same thing. From a mathematical perspective, the number of unique permutations for a subset of size r from a set of n items is as follows:

$$\text{Permutations} = P(n, r) = \frac{n!}{(n-r)!} \qquad \text{(Eq. 3-14)}$$

As an example of permutations, consider a combination lock with a dial, having forty digits. There is a 3-digit combination to this lock, and the three digits must be unique. We have a set of size forty, and a subset of size three. Using equation 3-14, we have 59,280 unique combinations. If you give the matter serious thought, the term "combination lock" is inappropriate – a "permutation lock" is more appropriate because ordering of the three digits is important.

3.4.4 Excel "Counts"

Fortunately, Microsoft Excel can help us with these combinatorial calculations. While the formulae presented above are helpful in making the appropriate calculations, Excel simplifies the process with the functions shown in Table 3.4

Excel Function	Purpose
=product(*data range*)	The product of all items in the data range
=factorial(*n*)	$n!$, or "n-factorial"
=combin(*n*, *r*)	$C(n, r)$ or $_nC_r$
=permut(*n*, *r*)	$P(n, r)$, or $_nP_r$

Table 3.4. Combinatorial Functions in Excel

3.5 Conclusions

As stated earlier, combinatorics and counting are topics that usually do not find coverage in introductory statistics books. In my opinion they are important because they tell us how many outcomes are possible, which is the "denominator" in probability calculations. Often this number is surprisingly large, which in turn reduces probability. Having this information is valuable, and can be helpful in any sort of organization have a better understanding of the environment in which they operate.

3.6 Exercises

1. I roll a pair of dice. Generate a table showing all possible outcomes and the probability of each outcome.
2. From the table above, what is the probability of rolling either a five or a nine?
3. Are the outcomes from Exercise 1 mutually exclusive? Why or why not?
4. Are the outcomes from Exercise 1 independent? Why or why not?
5. From a standard deck of 52 cards, what is the probability I draw a card of the Spades suit?
6. From a standard deck of 52 cards, what is the probability I draw a ten?

7. Using your answers from problems 5 and 6, what is the probability you draw a 10 of Spades? Does this answer make sense?

8. From a standard deck of 52 cards, what is the probability I draw a five or six?

9. Tonight the Houston Astros play at the New York Yankees. Analysts give the Yankees a 59% chance of winning. The Chicago Cubs play at the Pittsburgh Pirates tonight as well. Analysts project Pittsburgh winning with a 55% probability. Ties are not allowed – a team will either win or lose the game. Using this information, what is the probability that both the Yankees and the Cubs win tonight?

10. Using the information from Exercise 9, what is the probability that either Houston or the Cubs win?

11. Using the information from Exercise 9, what is the probability that neither the Yankees nor Pirates will win?

12. I recently collected some data about people's preference between retailers Wal-Mart and Target. 103 men preferred Target while 67 men preferred Wal-Mart. 158 women preferred Target while 27 preferred Wal-Mart. Using this information, what percent of those surveyed preferred Target?

13. Using the information from Exercise 12, what percent of those surveyed were men?

14. Using the information from Exercise 12, what percent of those surveyed were women that preferred Wal-Mart?

15. Using the information from Exercise 12, of all women, what percent preferred Target?

16. Using the information from Exercise 12, what percent were men given those that preferred Wal-Mart?

17. Can you draw any general conclusions from the information in Exercise 12?

18. Given the pizza data in Table 3.3, how many pizza combinations are possible if up to two toppings were permitted? Assume double-toppings on any single item (such as double pepperoni) is not permitted.

19. Given the pizza data in Table 3.3, how many pizza combinations are possible if up to two toppings were permitted? Assume double-toppings on any single item (such as double pepperoni) are permitted.

20. I have 15 photos. I have been asked to submit 4 of them for a family photo album. How many photo combinations are possible?
21. I have to visit 10 cities exactly once. The city from which I start my tour must the city in which I end my tour. How many different tours are possible?
22. I am giving an exam to 100 students. I am giving awards to the first, second and third place scorers. How many award scenarios are possible?

4. Random Variables

Probability and statistics can be described in many ways. Dealing with uncertainty is one aspect of the science. There are things in nature of which we never know with certainty. The closing daily stock price of a company, the monthly sales of a specific chemical and legal issues can all be considered sources of uncertainty. We refer to these types of things as **random variables**. Random variables are entities having values that we don't know with certainty. Perhaps we have a general idea of their behavior, but we cannot say with certainty what the outcome will be.

Consider a company's stock price. Today the company's stock price is $10/share. It seems reasonable to think that at this time tomorrow, the company's stock price will be similar to what it is today – perhaps slightly less than $10/share, perhaps slightly more than $10/share. The stock price at the end of a day's trading can be thought of as a random variable. Our hope is to gain an understanding of the random variable in terms of expectation and variation, so that we can make more informed strategic decision regarding all matters related to the random variable of interest.

This chapter evaluates the different types of random variables and describes their properties.

4.1 Discrete Random Variables

A discrete random variable has a finite number of outcomes, and these possible outcome values are known. Consider the roll of a pair of dice. The smallest possible outcome is a two (a pair of ones), and the largest possible outcome is a twelve (a pair of sixes). In total, there are eleven possible outcomes. Each possible outcome has some probability of occurring, and we assume that these probabilities are known.

4.1.1 Discrete Distribution

A specific outcome value of a discrete distribution is referred to as x, and the probability of x occurring is $P(x)$. These probabilities are known. The number of possible outcomes is n. The expected value of a random variable ($\mu = E(x)$), and its standard deviation ($\sigma = std(x)$) are determined as follows:

$$\mu = E(x) = \sum_{i=1}^{n} x_i P(x_i) \qquad \text{(Eq. 4-1)}$$

$$\sigma = \text{std}(x) = \sqrt{\sum_{i=1}^{n}(x_i - \mu)^2 P(x_i)}, \qquad \text{(Eq. 4-2)}$$

where x_i represents the value of outcome i. It is also worth noting that the cumulative probability through the ith possible outcome $\Sigma P(x_i)$ is simply the following:

$$\Sigma P(x_i) = \sum_{j=1}^{i} P(x_j) \qquad \text{(Eq. 4-3)}$$

Consider an example where a middle-school kid sells newspapers downtown before school. He sells the papers by the "bundle." Any given day he can sell as few as no bundles (x = 0) and as many as six bundles (x = 6). Table 4.1 shows the possible outcomes along with the associated probabilities and cumulative probabilities:

Bundles Sold	P(x)	$\Sigma P(x_i)$
0	.02	0.02
1	.08	0.10
2	.20	0.30
3	.35	0.65
4	.25	0.90
5	.07	0.97
6	.03	1.00

Table 4.1. Newspaper Sales Probabilities

Using the above equations, the kid can expect to sell 3.06 newspapers with a standard deviation of 1.22 newspapers. Figure 4.1 shows both the probability distribution and cumulative probability distributions for the seven possible outcomes. The cumulative probability distribution can be interpreted by stating the associated outcome *or less* has a probability of occurring equal to that particular cumulative probability value. For example, the cumulative probability value of 0.90 is associated with four bundles sold. This means that there is a 0.90 probability that 4 bundles or less will be sold.

Figure 4.1. Probability and Cumulative Distribution of Newspapers Sold

4.1.2   Binomial Distribution

The binomial distribution is a special type of discrete distribution. For each trial, the binomial distribution will result in one of two possible outcomes. The flip of a coin is binomial – either heads or tails will be the result. Consider a stock price – at the end of the day, the stock price will either gain value, or it will not gain value. Using the binomial distribution properties, we can model some specific number of successes (k) over some number of trials (n) given the probability of success (p). Once we know the value of p, we can use its complement to determine the probability of not having success (q, which is 1 - p).

There is a formula available to us that helps us determine the probability of k of successes given a binomial distribution over n trials, with a probability of success, p. The formula is as follows:

$$P(k) = \frac{n!}{(n-k)!k!}p^k q^{n-k} \qquad \text{(Eq. 4-4)}$$

Clearly, the above formula is intimidating. The combinatorial object preceding the probability shows the number of combinations of k successes, given the probability of success, p. Fortunately, Excel has a built-in function to perform the probability calculation for k successes over n trials of a binomial distribution. This function is as follows: "=binom.dist(k, n, p, FALSE)," where

"FALSE" asks for the probability values – "TRUE" asks for the cumulative probability values.

Let us consider an example of the human resources variety. A human resources manager is evaluated by senior management. Part of the performance review is based upon the tenure of the hires under her leadership. A hire is considered a "success" if they stay with the company for three or more years. As such, at the annual review of the HR manager, the hires from three years earlier are examined – if a hire from three years ago is still with the company it is considered a success. Otherwise, the hire is considered unsuccessful. Generally speaking, there is a 65% probability that a hire from three years ago is still with the company. Let's consider ten hires from three years ago ($n = 10$). Using the binomial distribution function, the probabilities of "successful" hires from three years ago are as follows:

Figure 4.2. Binomial Distribution Example

From Figure 4.2, we can see details of the probability of successful hires from three years ago. From this table, cumulative and inverse cumulative distribution functions can be determined to ask additional questions.

4.2 Continuous Random Variables

The probability distributions described above have a finite number of outcomes. Continuous probability distributions have an infinite number of possible outcomes. While there are many probability distributions to consider, we will examine the uniform distribution and the normal distribution.

4.2.1 Uniform Distribution

The uniform distribution has some minimum possible value, and some maximum possible value. All values between these two extreme values are equally likely to occur.

The random number generator on your calculator is an example of a uniform distribution. When you ask for a random number, you will get some number between 0 and 1. The number will never be less than 0 nor greater than 1. Using the "=rand()" function in Excel will produce the same result. If we generated an infinite number of random numbers via our calculator or in Excel, our histogram would look like this:

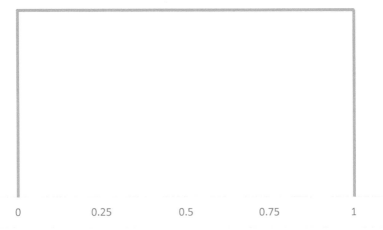

Figure 4.3. Uniform Distribution of a Simple Random Number Generator

Note that Figure 4.3 shows all values between 0 and 1 to occur with equal probability.

In truth, the uniform distribution is rarely seen to occur in nature, and is therefore, rarely studied. Its main value is we can simulate scores from a uniform distribution as an input to simulating more complex distributions, such as the normal distribution.

4.2.2 Normal Distribution

The normal distribution is the most important distribution of all. It is often seen in nature. We witness the normal distribution all of the time. The distribution of someone's height or weight, distribution of test scores, the distribution of how much sleep someone got last night, etc. To speak frankly, the normal distribution is a powerful force in nature – the distribution of many things follow a normal distribution. In plotting the normal distribution, the independent variable is "z," the number of standard deviations from the mean. The dependent variable is f(z), the probability, or density function associated with z. In more practical terms, "z" can be thought of as an outcome, whereas f(z) can be thought of as the probability associated with that particular outcome. The mathematical relationship between z and its density function is as follows:

$$f(z) = \frac{1}{\sqrt{2\pi}} e^{\frac{-z^2}{2}}$$ (Eq. 4-5)

Clearly, this is a complex calculation. Fortunately, Excel can help us generate a normally distributed plot via the function "=norm.dist(μ, σ, z, FALSE)," where μ is the population mean, σ is the population standard deviation, z is the given z-score, or number of standard deviations from the mean, and "FALSE" asks for the density function, or probability function as opposed to the cumulative density function ("TRUE").

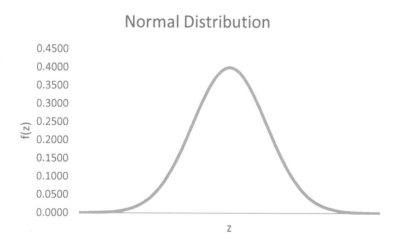

Figure 4.4. The Normal Distribution

The above formula provides us with a z-score, which can then be used to determine probabilities.

It is important to ask probabilistic questions when given a mean and standard deviation of a normally distributed population. The z-score, or number of standard deviations some given value x is from the population mean, μ, is given as follows:

$$z = \frac{x - \mu}{\sigma} \qquad \text{(Eq. 4-6)}$$

This formula "standardizes" the normal distribution to having a mean of 0 and a standard deviation of 1. The resultant z-score simply provides the distance between x and μ in units of standard deviations.

This z-score can then be used to determine the area under the curve to the "left" of z, or more specifically, the area under the curve between $-\infty$ and z, which is the integral of Eq. 4-5. Eq. 4-5 cannot be integrated by conventional means, so a numerical method must be used. Fortunately, Excel has provided a function for this. The "normsdist(z)" function provides the area under the normal curve to the left of the z-score. Figure 4.5 illustrates this, where "p" represents the area to the left of the z-score.

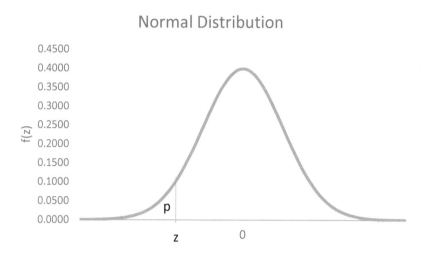

Figure 4.5. z-scores Associated with the Normal Distribution

For example, if we have an exam score having a population mean of 83 with a standard deviation of 5, an exam score of 87 would result in a z-score of 0.80, and an area under the curve of "normsdist(0.80)," which is 0.7881. In other words, the students with scores of 87 did better than 78.81% of the students in the population, also implying they did worse than (100% - 78.81%) 21.19% of the students on the exam.

Conversely, we might also wish to know the exam score associated with some specific percentile. There are tools available to help us with this calculation. First of all, the "normsinv(p)" function returns the z-score associated with the area under the curve equal to p, where the area is to the left of the z-score. Once we have the z-score, we can used Eq. 4-6 to get the actual value x associated with the z-score.

$$x = \mu + z\sigma \qquad\qquad\text{(Eq. 4-7)}$$

Of course, this equation is simply a re-arrangement of Eq. 4-6, where we solve for some specific value x.

Continuing with the same example as before, suppose we are interested in finding the exam score associated with the 75th percentile. This would mean the area under the curve, p, is 0.75, and the normsinv(p) function returns a z-score of 0.6745. Using this z-score along with a μ of 83 and a σ of 5, Eq. 4-5 gives us an x of 86.37.

4.3 The Central Limit Theorem

A large part of the remainder of this book relates to gathering sample data from a larger population. When we do this, we are attempting to say something interesting about the population as a whole. It just so happens that the distribution in which we sample most often resembles a normal distribution. This is the essence of the **Central Limit Theorem**. The Central Limit Theorem basically states that when we sample from a population, our findings resemble a normal distribution, and with larger sample sizes, the distribution becomes more defined and more accurately represents the population's distribution.

Figure 4.6 below shows this graphically. Panel (a) shows a histogram as the result of sampling from a population with a sample size of $n = 10$. Panel (b) shows the histogram as the result of sampling from the same population with a sample size of $n = 100$. Panels (c) and (d) show the same, but with sample sizes of 1,000 and 10,000. As one can see, increasing the sample size better resembles the population, providing us with less "predictive error."

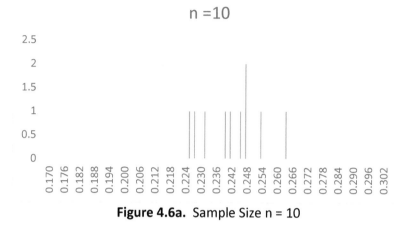

Figure 4.6a. Sample Size n = 10

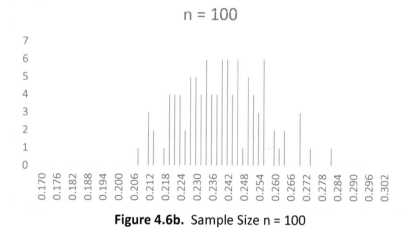

Figure 4.6b. Sample Size n = 100

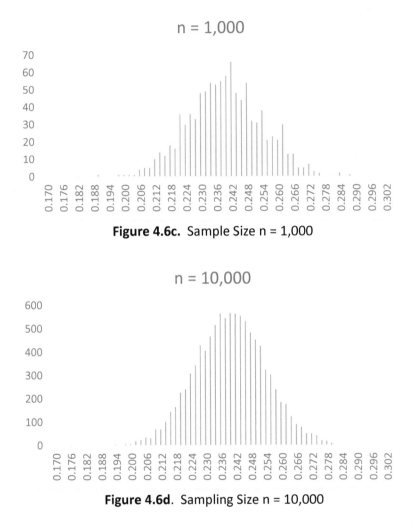

Figure 4.6c. Sample Size n = 1,000

Figure 4.6d. Sampling Size n = 10,000

The "predictive error" as stated above is a bit nebulous. It intends to describe our general ability to understand the population. As one can see from Figure 4.6, larger sample sizes are better in helping us understand the population. We can quantify this phenomenon via the standard error measurement:

$$\text{Standard Error (se)} = s/\sqrt{n}, \qquad \text{(Eq. 4-8)}$$

where s is the sample standard deviation, and n is the sample size. As one can see, our standard error decreases with larger sample sizes.

The standard error is used to quantify the **sampling distribution**. The sampling distribution is a normal distribution, but is adjusted for the sample size we are using. The t-statistic is used to represent the distance between our sample mean ($\bar{x}$) and the a priori population mean (μ) in units of standard errors. Mathematically, this is as follows:

$$t = \frac{\bar{x} - \mu}{s/\sqrt{n}}$$
(Eq. 4-9)

This particular equation has no application at this point in the book, but it will when we explore hypothesis testing. At this point, it is reasonable just to understand that the t-statistic is the result of sampling, and its value simply represents how many standard errors our sample mean is from the population mean.

4.4 Conclusions

Despite the fact that many different types of probability distributions were covered in this chapter, we have only scratched the surface in terms of the multitude of probability that exist in nature. Fortunately, the normal distribution is a powerful force in nature, and this particular distribution serves us well for the remainder of this book.

Additionally, the discrete distributions also occur frequently and we now have the ability to better understand them.

4.5 Exercises

1. I roll a single die. What is the expected value of the outcome?
2. I roll a single die. What is the standard deviation associated with the outcome?

Use the information provided in Problem 3 below to address questions 3 – 7.

3. I buy 16 tropical fish of the species "cichlisoma negrofasciata." I cannot determine the gender of the fish, but I'm told there is a 53% probability of a single fish being a female. Construct the appropriate probability distribution, with outcomes of 0 females to 16 females.
4. What is the probability of there being six or fewer females?

5. What is the probability of there being more than nine females?
6. What is the expected number of females?
7. What is the standard deviation of the number of females?

Use the following information to address questions 8 – 12. The population of American males have an average height of 70 inches, with a standard deviation of 1.5 inches.

8. What is the probability of a male having a height of 72 inches or more?
9. What is the probability of a male being 68 inches or shorter?
10. What is the probability of a male being between 69 and 71 inches?
11. What height is associated with the 85th percentile?
12. What height is associated with the 25th percentile?

5. Estimation

We have stated many times that statistics involves using sample data to say things about the population. This will be said many more times before you finish this book. This adage is especially true in this chapter. Here, we wish to articulate a population characteristic based on sample data. Given that we are saying something about the population with incomplete data, we are taking a leap of faith, so to speak. In short, we are *estimating* a population parameter. However, the **confidence interval** helps us articulate how confident we are in our estimate of this particular population parameter.

5.1 Means

Estimating the population mean (μ), via sample data is the first order of business. When we gather sample data, we know the sample size (n), and we can calculate the sample mean ($\bar{x}$) and sample standard deviation (s). We can use this data, along with the appropriate t-statistic to construct a confidence interval, providing a lower bound (*LB*) and an upper bound (*UB*) of our estimate of μ. When this boundary is established, we state a certain level of confidence that the true population mean lies within the specified boundary. The level of confidence we have in this interval, or boundary is $1 - \alpha$, where the value of α is either given or assumed. The value of α it typically referred to as the **level of significance** and is an input into the size of the boundaries of the interval. Mathematically, this interval is as follows:

$$P(LB \leq \mu \leq UB) = 1 - \alpha \qquad \text{(Eq. 5-1)}$$

In essence, Eq. 5-1 is telling us that we are ($1 - \alpha$) confident that the true population mean is between the lower and upper boundaries. We can re-write Eq. 5-1 so that the statistics associated with our sample data are shown:

$$P(\bar{x} - t_{\alpha/2}\frac{s}{\sqrt{n}} \leq \mu \leq \bar{x} + t_{\alpha/2}\frac{s}{\sqrt{n}}) = 1 - \alpha. \qquad \text{(Eq. 5-2)}$$

Here, the value of $t_{\alpha/2}$ represents the distance, expressed via the number of standard errors, our boundary is from the population mean. This value is often referred to as the "**half-width.**" Excel provides us this value via the following function:

$$t_{\alpha/2} = \text{t.inv.2t}(\alpha, n - 1) \qquad \text{(Eq. 5-3)}$$

This particular value is also used in hypothesis testing for means, covered in the next chapter.

For convenience, the lower and upper boundaries are often shown in the following compressed notation:

$$\bar{x} \pm t_{\alpha/2} \frac{s}{\sqrt{n}} \qquad \text{(Eq. 5-4)}$$

Here, the "±" symbol show that we are both subtracting and adding the specified number of standard errors from and to our sample mean, $\bar{x}$.

As an example, let's assume that we are interested in a 95% confidence interval estimate of a company's annual salary increases to their employees. We do not have salary increase information for the entire payroll, so we need to randomly select workers and ask them about their annual salary increase. Our random sampling effort resulting in 25 participants ($n = 25$), resulting in a sample mean of an $1,800 annual increase, with a standard deviation of $475. Because we are seeking a 95% confidence interval, our value of $\alpha = 0.05$. Using the appropriate Excel function as shown in Eq. 5-3, we have a $t_{\alpha/2}$ value of 2.06. Substituting these values into Eq. 5-4, we have the following:

$$1,800 \pm (2.06)\frac{475}{\sqrt{25}} \qquad \text{(Eq. 5-5)}$$

This results in a lower bound of $1603.93 and an upper bound of $1996.07. We can then formally state our findings as follows:

$$P(\$1603.93 \leq \mu \leq \$1996.07) = 0.95 \qquad \text{(Eq. 5-6)}$$

In words, this is stated as follows: *we are 95% confident that our true population mean salary increase is between $1603.93 and $1996.07.*

5.2 Proportions

We can also estimate proportions via confidence intervals. In this context, a **proportion** is the percent of a sample that meets some criterion. Proportions are often used in understanding consumer preferences, as well as in political science, where we try to gain a better understanding of where candidates stand in terms of voters.

To estimate proportions, we must first define a few terms, which are provided in Table 5.1.

Term	Explanation
$\hat{p}$	Estimate of the population proportion
p	Population Proportion
n	Sample Size
$z_{\alpha/2}$	Half-Width of Interval

Table 5.1. Values for Proportion Confidence Interval

The confidence interval for proportions is very similar to that of the confidence interval for means. We add and subtract the standard error times the half-width to and from the estimate. The standard error is as follows:

$$se = \sqrt{\frac{\hat{p}(1-\hat{p})}{n}} \qquad \text{(Eq. 5-7)}$$

Using notation similar to that from Eq. 5-4, our confidence interval is as follows:

$$\hat{p} \pm z_{\alpha/2}\sqrt{\frac{\hat{p}(1-\hat{p})}{n}} \qquad \text{(Eq. 5-8)}$$

The similarities between Eq. 5-8 and Eq. 5-4 are pretty obvious, but there is one major difference that needs to be discussed. The confidence interval for means exploits a t-distribution because we are sampling from a population – this seems consistent with what was discussed in Section 4.3. The confidence interval for a proportion, however, exploits a z-distribution, despite the fact that we are sampling from a population – this seems counter-intuitive.

The reason that we exploit a z-distribution instead of a t-distribution for a proportion confidence interval is because we assume a large sample size for a proportion confidence interval, which would force t-scores to essentially equal z-scores. It has also been discovered that confidence for proportions are only reliable for larger sample sizes, hence the reason for using the z-distribtion.

The z-score that provides us with the half-width for a proportion confidence interval is provided by the following Excel function:

$$z_{\alpha/2} = \text{normsinv}(1-\alpha/2) \qquad \text{(Eq. 5-9)}$$

Let's look at an example of how to construct a confidence interval for a proportion. Let's assume that we administered a taste-test to a group of 1,572 people. Of the people sampled, 832 of them preferred Brand A over Brand B. This means that the estimated proportion of people who preferred Brand A over B is $\hat{p}$ = 832/1572, which equals 0.5292. If we desire a 99% confidence interval, then α = 0.01. Using Eq. 5-9 to obtain the z-score, we have $z_{\alpha/2}$ equal to 2.5758. Substituting these values into Eq. 5-8, we the following confidence interval:

$$P(0.4968 \le p \le 0.5617) = 0.99 \qquad \text{(Eq. 5-10)}$$

Another way of saying the above is that there is a 99% probability that the true proportion of consumers preferring Brand A over B is between 0.4968 and 0.5617.

5.3 Differences between means

The last type of confidence interval we cover is the confidence interval for the difference between two means. Here, we are actually sampling from two populations and constructing a confidence interval based upon the differences in their expected values. For this exercise, we introduce some new, but familiar terms in Table 5.2.

Quantity	Sample 1	Sample 2
Sample Size	n_1	n_2
Population Mean	μ_1	μ_2
Sample Mean	$\bar{x}_1$	$\bar{x}_2$
Sample Standard Deviation	s_1	s_2

Table 5.2. Values Used for Difference Between Means Confidence Interval

The standard error for this confidence interval is as follows:

$$se = \sqrt{\frac{s_1^2}{n_1} + \frac{s_2^2}{n_2}}$$

(Eq. 5-11)

The degrees of freedom are as follows:

$$df = \frac{\left(\frac{s_1^2}{n_1} + \frac{s_2^2}{n_2}\right)^2}{\left(\frac{1}{n_1 - 1}\right)\left(\frac{s_1^2}{n_1}\right)^2 + \left(\frac{1}{n_2 - 1}\right)\left(\frac{s_2^2}{n_2}\right)^2}$$

(Eq. 5-12)

The formula for the confidence interval of the difference between two population means is as follows:

$$(\bar{x}_1 - \bar{x}_2) \pm t_{\alpha/2}\sqrt{\frac{s_1^2}{n_1} + \frac{s_2^2}{n_2}}$$

(Eq. 5-13)

Here, the $t_{\alpha/2}$ value is the same as it was as stated in Eq. 5-3.

As an example, let us construct a 90% confidence interval ($\alpha = 0.10$) for the difference in average exam scores administered to two different classes. The following data is provided:

Quantity	Sample 1	Sample 2
Sample Size	$n_1 = 47$	$n_2 = 52$
Sample Mean	$\bar{x}_1 = 81$	$\bar{x}_2 = 83.5$
Sample Standard Deviation	$s_1 = 7.2$	$s_2 = 6.2$

Table 5.3. Example Data for Difference in Average Exam Scores

Using the given values and formulae, our confidence interval is as follows:

$$P(-4.76 \le \mu_1 - \mu_2 \le -0.24) = 0.90 \qquad \text{(Eq. 5-14)}$$

In other words, the difference in population means between the two classes is between -4.75 and -0.25.

5.4 Conclusions

Generating confidence intervals is simply a way to estimate values associated with a population. The more confident we need to be, the wider the interval must be. As the same time, if we use as a large a sample size as possible, the width of our intervals with narrow.

Problems of this type become very helpful when we pursue two-tailed tests of hypotheses in the next chapter. Because of this, the next chapter, which has substantial content is eased a bit because of this chapter.

5.5 Exercises

1. The "NFLLinemen" data set contains data on the weight of randomly sampled offensive lineman in the National Football League. Using $\alpha = 0.01$, construct the appropriate confidence interval for the population mean.

2. Using $\alpha = 0.05$, construct a confidence interval on the pulse rates of randomly selected university athletes. The data set is provided in the "PulseRate" file.

3. I randomly sampled 2,234 North Carolinians on whether or not they considered Wake Forest University the best school in the state. 1,465 respondents did consider Wake Forest the best school in the state. Construct a 95% confidence interval to estimate the true proportion of those who think Wake Forest is the best school in the state.

4. 3,689 Oregonians were randomly asked if they support legalization of marijuana for medicinal purposes. 2,983 people responded in the affirmative. Using this data to construct a 93% confidence interval to estimate the true proportion of Oregonians that support legalization of marijuana for medicinal purposes.

5. Professor Fraud and Professor Quick both teach separate sections of Principles of Finance. They gave the same exam to the students. The "FinanceProfessors" data set provides the exam scores for both sections. Use this data to construct a 90% confidence interval on the difference between the two sections.

6. Is one professor better than the other? Why or why not?

7. A food company just came up with two new products for diabetics: Product X and Product Y. They are concerned about the amount of carbohydrates in the product, as diabetics need to be careful about carbohydrate intake. The file "DiabeticFoods" contains carbohydrate data (in grams) for randomly selected items of the two different products. Construct a 96% confidence interval for the difference in carbohydrates between the two products.

8. Regardless of the type of confidence interval constructed, what does a wide confidence interval suggest?

9. Regardless of the type of confidence interval constructed, what does a narrow confidence interval suggest?

10. What is the margin of error in Problem 3?

11. What is the margin of error in Problem 4?

6. Hypothesis Testing

In science or commerce, we are not permitted to make unsubstantiated claims. For example, if I work for an electronics firm, I cannot tell my colleagues and managers the following: "our Q55 electronic switches cannot handle a 25-volt load." What is wrong with this question? We have made a claim without any evidence of formal scientific testing. In order to make a reasonable claim outside of a pub, we need to support the claim with scientific proof of the claim's authenticity. To provide the scientific proof, we need to conduct a formal hypothesis test.

This chapter provides us the tools to make hypothesis tests. We will test hypotheses involving means, proportions and differences between means. In other words, we extend the work from the previous chapter with the intent of affirming a disproving a claim.

6.1 General Process

A hypothesis is a **claim**, **inference** or **conjecture**. These terms are used interchangeably. Chapter 6 of this book is called "**Hypothesis Testing**," while other books might use "**Statistical Inference**." Regardless of the terminology used, we are testing a claim about the population to see if it is supported by scientific proof. Determining whether or not a claim is true requires a formal hypothesis test.

These tests take on three different types. The first type of test is interested in whether or not a population parameter is equal to some specific value vs. *not equal to* some value. The second type of test is concerned with determining whether or not some population parameter is equal to some value vs. *less than* some value. The third type of test is concerned with whether or not some population parameter is equal to some value vs. *greater than* some value. These three types of tests are formalized in the subsequent sections.

6.1.1 Null and Alternative Hypotheses

Each hypothesis test involves two different hypotheses: the **null hypothesis (H_0)** and the **alternative hypothesis (H_A)**. These two hypotheses are stated at the same time.

The null hypothesis test is a benign hypothesis and states the status quo – it states what is typically regarded as true. Here is an example of a null hypothesis: the average weight of a box of Cheerios is 14 ounces. Mathematically, we would state this as follows:

$$H_0: \mu = 14 \qquad \text{(Eq. 6-1)}$$

Note that the population mean is involved in H_0. This is the case because the H_0 is making a claim about the population. Also note that equality is involved – the H_0 will always involve equality, because we are claiming the status quo. Finally, we should note that when making our conclusions about a hypothesis, we always base our conclusion on the H_0: we will either *reject* H_0, or *fail to reject* H_0.

The alternative hypothesis, H_A, contradicts H_0. H_A says something of interest involving inequality. H_A is typically the direct question in which the researcher/investigator is most interested. As stated earlier, there are three types of H_A: one that states "not equal to;" one that states "less than;" and another stating "more than." The H_A is where the "burden of proof" lies. H_A must provide evidence beyond a reasonable doubt that the H_0 is incorrect. If a criminal trial comes to mind via this description, you are definitely on the right track: we assume H_0 is true (innocence) unless proven otherwise (guilt is proven beyond a reasonable doubt). This brings us to potential errors. As is the case with a criminal trial, we can make mistakes in our decision regarding H_0. A Type I Error occurs with the probability of α, while the probability of a Type II Error occurs with the probability of β. Table 6.1 explores these possible errors.

	Reject H_0	Do Not Reject H_0
H_0 True	Type I Error	Correct Decision
H_0 False	Correct Decision	Type II Error

Table 6.1. Outcomes from H_0 Decisions

The first type of H_A we discuss is the "not equal to" variety. When presented alongside H_0 in our Cheerios example, we have the following:

$$H_0: \mu = 14; H_A: \mu \neq 14 \qquad \text{(Eq. 6-2)}$$

Not equal to implies inequality – we do not specifically consider which type of inequality (neither "<" nor ">"). One might wonder who might be interested in this scenario. One possible answer, in the context of this example, would be the quality control people who make the Cheerios. They simply wish to consistently fill the boxes with 14 ounces of cereal. Figure 6-1 shows this scenario graphically with regard to the population mean. The shaded areas are referred to as the "reject regions." Because the H_A states "not equal to," we have a "<" reject region and a ">" reject region. Because we have reject regions on both sides of the distribution, we call this a "two-tail test."

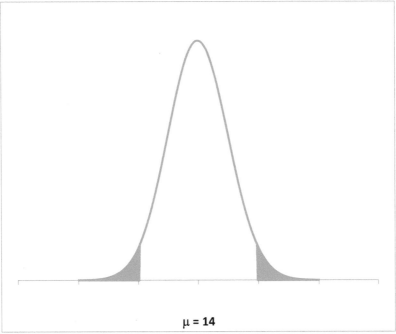

$\mu = 14$

Figure 6-1. H_0: $\mu = 14$; H_A: $\mu \neq 14$

The second type of H_A is the "less than" hypothesis. In the context of our Cheerios example, we would say the following:

$$H_0: \ \mu = 14; \ H_A: \ \mu < 14 \qquad \text{(Eq. 6-3)}$$

For this example, an interested party might be consumer advocates who wish to expose Cheerios for "skimping" on the amount of Cheerios they put into their boxes, in the event that H_A is true. Figure 6-2 graphically shows this scenario, with the reject region on the left-hand side. Because we have reject region on just one side of the distribution, we call this a "one-tail test."

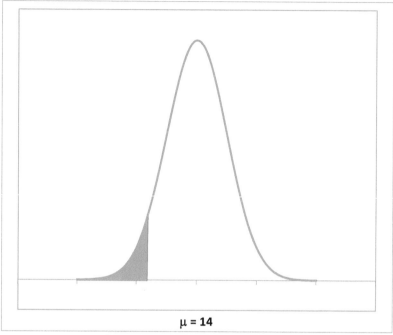

μ = 14

Figure 6.2. H_0: μ = 14; H_A: μ < 14

The last type of H_A we explore is the "greater than" scenario. Continuing with our Cheerios example, we have the following:

$$H_0: μ = 14; H_A: μ > 14 \qquad \text{(Eq. 6-4)}$$

For this particular scenario, senior executives at General Mills (the company who makes Cheerios) might be interested because if H_A were true, cereal would be given away, which is an unforgivable offense in the eyes of senior management and shareholders. Figure 6-3 shows this scenario, where you will note the reject region is on the right hand side. Because we have reject region on just one side of the distribution, we call this a "one-tail test."

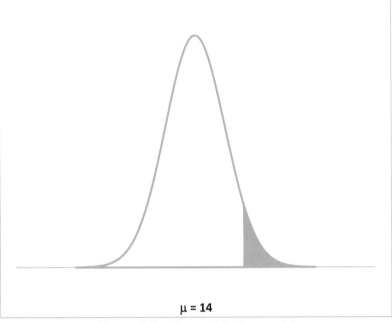

μ = 14

Figure 6-3. H₀: μ = 14; Hₐ: μ > 14

·With the general concepts of H_0 and H_A now stated, it is time to discuss the steps of hypothesis testing.

6.1.2   Steps of the Hypothesis Test

Students often consider hypothesis testing the most difficult aspect of statistics – that was certainly the case for me. However, with practice (and a good teacher), the following steps of the process become second nature.

6.1.2.1   Constructing H₀ and Hₐ

Properly constructing H_0 and H_A are the most difficult part of the process. It is important to note that the instructor has a very large responsibility here in clearly writing the questions. Have a look at the following hypothetical questions:

a) The quality control department at Cheerios is concerned about putting 14 ounces of cereal into the boxes. If they put too few Cheerios into the box, customers are not getting their money's worth. If they put too much cereal into the boxes, General Mills loses money.

As such, putting 14 ounces of cereal into the boxes is supremely important. Using the "Cheerios" data set, please determine if General Mills is putting the proper amount of cereal in the boxes.

b) The DeliveryGuys parcel service claims a delivery time of less than 6 hours. Using the "DeliveryGuys" data set, please determine if their claim is true.

c) CircuitKings makes circuit boards for TV remote controls. They use a silver alloy for conductivity. Each circuit board should contain .25mg of the silver alloy. If more than this amount of the alloy is used, CircuitKings loses money because the silver alloy is very expensive. CircuitKings is worried that they are putting too much of the alloys in their circuit boards. Using the CircuitKings data set, please determine if they are putting too much silver alloy in their circuit boards.

Each of these statements are fair and clearly written. Statement "a" should result in H_A being of the "$\neq$" variety, because the dangers of putting too little cereal into the box is just as bad as putting too much cereal into the box. Statement "b" should result in H_A being of the "<" variety because a direct claim is made implying as much. In this case, the H_A is explicitly stated, which occasionally happens. Statement "c" is of the ">" variety because the dangers of putting too much of the silver alloy is discussed. In summary, then, we have the following hypotheses ready for testing:

a) H_0: $\mu = 14$; H_A: $\mu \neq 14$
b) H_0: $\mu = 6$; H_A: $\mu < 6$
c) H_0: $\mu = 0.25$; H_A: $\mu > 0.25$

There are two important rules to remember here. First, the H_0 always involves equality – writing H_0 is easy. Second, the H_A always involves inequality. Another important thing to remember is that the H_A is more interesting than the benign H_0. A final noteworthy item is that if you find the problem not clearly written, where the "inequality" is vaguely worded, a "$\neq$" H_A is probably the best choice.

For this section, we will use scenario "a" above as our example:

$$H_0: \mu = 14; H_A: \mu \neq 14$$

Additionally for this example, we will use $\alpha = 0.05$, and the Cheerios data set, which contains 25 observed weights of randomly-selected Cheerios boxes claiming to be 14 ounces.

6.1.2.2   Defining the Reject Region

When performing hypothesis testing, you will either be given a value of α or you will need to assume one. Typically, on homework assignments and exams, α should be given. On written assignments of a "case-based" nature, it is reasonable to have the student assume a value of α. The value of α determines the size of the reject region – it is as simple as that. If α is small, then the reject region is small. If α is large, then the reject region is large. In figures 6-1 – 6-3, the values of α are represented by the shaded areas, which comprise the reject region. We use the "t.inv" functions in Excel to obtain the critical value associated with α. Inputting α and the degrees of freedom (df) in the t.inv function, we get an output of the critical value, defining the reject region.

H_A Type	Excel Function
$\neq$	+/- t.inv.2t(α, n-1)
<	t.inv(α, n-1)
>	t.inv(1-α, n-1)

Table 6.2. Excel Functions for Reject Regions

This critical value will be compared with the test-statistic (discussed next) to determine whether or not H_0 should be rejected.

Regarding our example, we use $\alpha = 0.05$ and t.inv.2t(0.05, 25 - 1), which results in a critical value of +/- 2.06. This value is both positive and negative because we are seeking a critical value for both tails.

There is one final comment that needs to made about the value of α. Students often ask what value of α should be used. This is a good question. A rule of thumb is to use $\alpha = 0.05$, but this varies across industries. The medical industry often uses value of 0.01 or lower. Lower values of α result in more conservative tests, while higher values of α result in more liberal tests. What this means is that conservative tests make it harder to reject H_0, while more liberal tests make it easier to reject H_0. If seeking a more liberal test, however, an α value exceeding 0.10 is considered inappropriate. Never use an α value in excess of 0.10.

6.1.2.3   Determining the Test Statistic

The critical value is compared to the test statistic. The test statistic is the result of the following formula, which was introduced in Chapter 5:

$$t = \frac{\bar{x} - \mu}{s/\sqrt{n}} \qquad \text{(Eq. 6-5)}$$

From the Cheerios data set, we have the following statistics: the sample mean ($\bar{x}$) is 14.03, with a sample standard deviation (s) of 0.1087. The data set contains $n = 25$ observations. We also have, of course, our hypothesized population mean of $\mu = 14$. Substituting these values into Eq. 6-5, we have the following test-statistic:

$$t = \frac{14.03 - 14}{0.1087/\sqrt{25}} = 1.51 \qquad \text{(Eq. 6-6)}$$

This value of 1.51 tells us that our sample mean is 1.51 standard errors above the hypothesized population mean. It is above the hypothesized population mean because it has a positive sign – in other words, $\bar{x}$ exceeds μ.

This test statistic is compared to the critical value, so that we can make a decision regarding H_0.

6.1.2.4   Decision Regarding H_0

As stated earlier, we compare the critical value(s) with the test statistic. Figure 6.4 shows the result of our test in a graphical sense. You will notice that our test statistic does not fall into the reject region – the shaded area. Because of this, we DO NOT reject H_0. As such, we do not have adequate evidence to say anything contrary to H_0. General Mills is in fact putting 14 ounces of cereal into the boxes. If the test statistic did fall into the reject region, we would reject H_0, and claim that General Mills is not putting 14 ounces of cereal into the boxes.

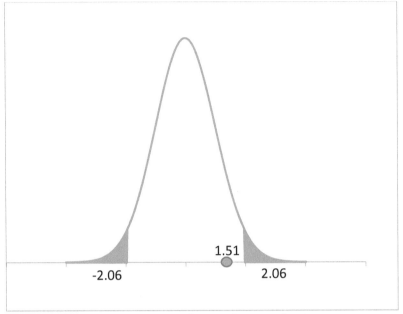

Figure 6.4. Results of Example Hypothesis Test

6.1.2.5 Calculating the p-value

The p-value of the test is the last thing we need to calculate. The p-value is the size of the reject region associated with the test statistic. Figure 6.5 shows us the p-value from a visual perspective.

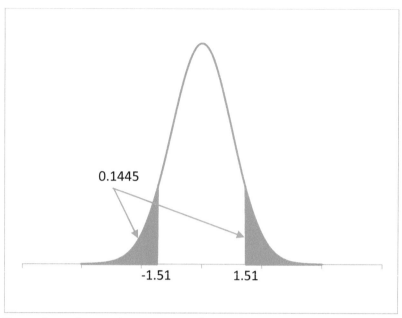

Figure 6.5. The p-value Associated with the Example Hypothesis Test

Because this is a two-tailed test, we must make the shaded region associated with the test-statistic two-tailed as well. In order for us to calculate the p-value, we must use the tdist functions, which are detailed in Table 6.3.

Number of Tails	Function
1-Tailed Test	tdist(|t|, n-1, 1)
2-Tailed Test	tdist(|t|, n-1, 2)

Table 6.3. Functions for p-value.

You will note that the p-value is greater than the value of α. This should be the case because we failed to reject H_0. If our test statistic found itself in the reject region, we would reject H_0, and our resultant p-value would be less than our value of α. If we already knew that we weren't going to reject H_0 in this example, why did we calculate the p-value? The answer to this question is because the p-value gives us more information – it tells us the "break-even" value that could be used for α – the point of indifference between rejecting and not rejecting H_0. If p is less than α, we reject H_0. If p is greater than α, we fail to reject H_0. Or more crudely put:

If the p is low, H_0 must go. If the p is high, H_0 will fly.

Comparisons between the p-value and α are not intended to confuse the student. I have noticed over the years that the adage above puts things in proper perspective for students. The p-value is more important than α, because the p-value can be compared to any threshold (α). In fact, statistical software packages don't even ask for values of α – they just return p-values. Figure 6.6 shows JMP output for our example problem – you will only see a p-value reported, nothing about the value of α.

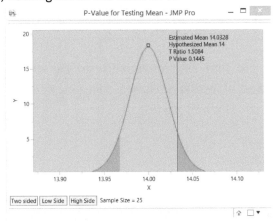

Figure 6.6. p-value Calculation via JMP

While not completely true from a technical standpoint, I like to think of the p-value of the test as the probability that the H_0 is true.[2]

6.2 Testing Means

Of course, the example problem we explored throughout the previous section was a test concerning means. There are also tests concerning proportions and differences between means. In this section, we will do another hypothesis test involving means.

For this example problem, we will consider the DeliveryGuys example,

---

[2] More specifically, the p-value is defined as *the probability of obtaining a result more extreme than what was observed, assuming H_0 is true*. "More extreme" means further into the reject region. It is my opinion it is reasonable to consider the p-value the probability of H_0 being true.

described in the previous section. As you recall, DeliveryGuys claim an average delivery time of less than six hours. This results in the following:

$$H_0: \mu = 6; H_A: \mu < 6$$

We will use the DeliveryGuys data set, containing $n = 40$ observations, and we will assume an $\alpha = 0.01$. Our descriptive statistics tell us that the sample mean ($\bar{x}$) is 5.89, and the sample standard deviation (s) is 0.2836. The hypothesized population mean is, of course, $\mu = 6$. Using t.inv(0.01, 40-1), we have a critical value of -2.43. Using Eq. 6-6 to calculate the t-statistic, we have the following:

$$t = \frac{5.89 - 6}{0.2836/\sqrt{40}} = -2.45 \qquad \text{(Eq. 6-7)}$$

Since the t-statistic is more extreme than the critical value, we reject H_0 and claim a delivery time of less than 6 hours. Figure 6-7 shows the relationship between the critical value and the test statistic.

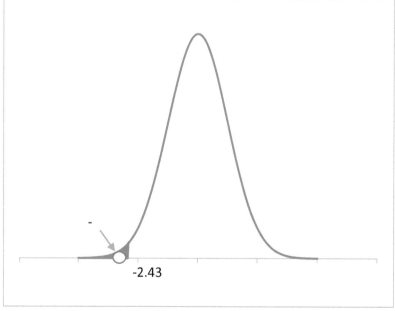

-2.43

Figure 6-7. Result of One-Tail Hypothesis Test

The test statistic falls into the reject region. Using the tdist function to calculate the p-value, we have the following:

$$\text{p-value} = \text{tdist}(|\text{-}2.45|, 40 - 1, 1) = 0.0094 \qquad \text{(Eq. 6-8)}$$

Note that our p-value above is less than $\alpha = 0.01$, supporting our decision to reject H_0.

It should be noted that Eq. 6-8 takes the absolute value of the t-statistic as an argument, because this function will return an error message if the t-statistic is negative. This caveat is also noted in Table 6-3.

6.3 Testing Proportions

The second type of hypothesis test we discuss relates to proportions: whether or not sampling provides us a value equal to some hypothesized value. As was the case with testing means, there are three different types of H_A: not equal to, less than and greater than. Unlike testing means, for testing proportions, we use the z-distribution instead of the t-distribution. The reason for this is because for testing proportions, we always assume a large sample size, rendering the t-distribution the same as the z-distribution. Because of this, our critical values, given some value of α are shown in Table 6-4.

H_A Type	Excel Function
$\neq$	+/- normsinv(1 - α/2)
<	normsinv(α)
>	normsinv(1 - α)

Table 6.4. Excel Functions for Proportion Test Reject Regions

Note that for the two-tailed test, our critical value takes on both +/- values. As a reminder from our coverage of confidence intervals for proportions, "$\hat{p}$" is our sample proportion, while "p" represents the true population proportion. Given this, our test statistic is shown in Eq. 6-9:

$$z = \frac{\hat{p} - p}{\sqrt{\dfrac{\hat{p}(1 - \hat{p})}{n}}} \qquad \text{(Eq. 6-9)}$$

:

$$H_0: p = 0.50; \ H_A: \ p > 0.50 \qquad \text{(Eq. 6-10)}$$

Because this is a one-tailed test, our critical values is "normsinv(1 - 0.03)," which is 1.88. Our value of $\hat{p}$ is 182/352 = .5170. This provides us with a test statistic of

$$z = \frac{0.5170 - 0.50}{\sqrt{\dfrac{0.5170(1 - 0.5170)}{352}}} = 0.64 \qquad \text{(Eq. 6-11)}$$

The test statistic does not fall into the reject region, so we fail to reject the H_0, as we do not have sufficient evidence to claim Keenan as the winner. Figure 6-8 shows this graphically

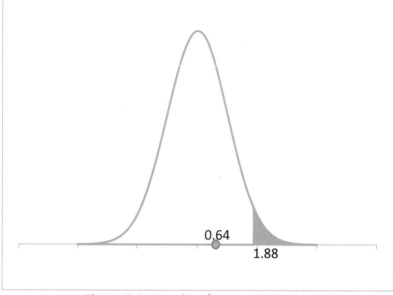

Figure 6-8. Results of Mayoral Election

In terms of the p-value for this type of test, we use the "normsdist" function. Depending on the type of H_A, we use the following functions:

H_A Type	Excel Function
$\neq$	2*(1-normsdist(-|z|))
<	normsdist(z)
>	1 – normsdist(z)

Table 6.5. Excel Functions for Proportion Test p-values

For this problem, our p-value is then $1 - \text{normsdist}(0.64)$, which is 0.2611.

The above problem brings up an issue that is relevant to everyday life. If you watch the news regarding politics and elections, you will see lots of polling. If you look at the details of the polling, you will sometimes see something like a "margin of error of +/- 3.5%." This "margin of error" that is referred to is simply what we call the standard error, $\sqrt{\hat{p}(1-\hat{p})/n}$. Smaller sample sizes result in larger "margins of error," which should make sense given what we have already learned about the central limit theorem.

Let us consider one other example. In the hot dog business, the USDA places an upper limit on variety meats that can be put into hot dogs. "Variety meats" are tongues, tails, snouts, etc. Hot dogs must have less than 5% variety meats. A local hot dog maker decides to test whether or not they are in compliance. They documented their last 200 batches, and found an average of 1.5% variety meats in them. At the $\alpha = 0.05$ level, are they in compliance?

Clearly, our hypotheses are as follows: H_0: $p = 0.05$; H_A: $p < 0.05$. Using normsinv(0.05), we have a critical value of -1.65 which defines the reject region. Using Eq. 6-9, our test statistic is as follows:

$$z = \frac{0.015 - 0.05}{\sqrt{\frac{0.015(1 - 0.015)}{200}}} = -4.07 \qquad \text{(Eq. 6-12)}$$

This test statistic is very small, and is in an extreme part of the reject region. When normsdist(-4.07) is used to find a p-value, a very small number may appear. In my case the number displayed was "2.33E-05." This means $(2.33)(10)^{-5}$, which a very small number. When this happens, we simply state that $p < 0.0001$.

6.4 Testing Differences between Means

There are times when we need to determine whether or not means from two different populations are the same. Additionally, there are times when we need to determine whether or not there is a *specific* difference in means from two different populations. We can do this via hypothesis testing. Before showing the appropriate calculations, we refresh your memory with some relevant terms.

Quantity	Sample 1	Sample 2
Sample Size	n_1	n_2
Population Mean	μ_1	μ_2
Sample Mean	$\bar{x}_1$	$\bar{x}_2$
Sample Standard Deviation	s_1	s_2

Table 6.6. Values Used for Difference Between Means

When we test from two different populations for equality of means, we can construct the following hypotheses:

$$H_0: (\mu_1 - \mu_2) = 0; \quad H_A: (\mu_1 - \mu_2) \neq 0 \qquad \text{(Eq. 6-13)}$$

For a specific different in means, we can use the following, where "d" represents the value of the specific difference:

$$H_0: (\mu_1 - \mu_2) = d; \quad H_A: (\mu_1 - \mu_2) \neq d \qquad \text{(Eq. 6-14)}$$

Both sets of hypotheses above are two-tailed tests, but one-tailed tests are also possible, where H_A: is of the "<" or ">" variety, although the one-tailed tests are not as common as the two-tailed tests. As with other tests, we are given or we assume a value for α. Table 6.6 shows the t.inv functions we use to determine critical values for reject regions:

H_A Type	Excel Function
$\neq$	+/- t.inv.2t(α, df)
<	t.inv(α, df)
>	t.inv(1-α, df)

Table 6.7. Excel Functions for Reject Regions

Here, the value for degrees of freedom, *df*, is as follows:

$$df = \frac{\left(\frac{s_1^2}{n_1} + \frac{s_2^2}{n_2}\right)^2}{\left(\frac{1}{n_1 - 1}\right)\left(\frac{s_1^2}{n_1}\right)^2 + \left(\frac{1}{n_2 - 1}\right)\left(\frac{s_2^2}{n_2}\right)^2} \qquad \text{(Eq. 6-15)}$$

The *general* test statistic for the difference between means is as follows:

$$t = \frac{(\bar{x}_1 - \bar{x}_2) - (\mu_1 - \mu_2)}{\sqrt{\dfrac{s_1^2}{n_1} + \dfrac{s_2^2}{n_2}}} \qquad \text{(Eq. 6-16)}$$

If we are testing for equality in means, Eq. 6-16 simplifies to the following, because equality of population means implies $\mu_1 = \mu_2$:

$$t = \frac{(\bar{x}_1 - \bar{x}_2)}{\sqrt{\dfrac{s_1^2}{n_1} + \dfrac{s_2^2}{n_2}}} \qquad \text{(Eq. 6-17)}$$

If we are testing for a specific difference in means equal to "d," where d = μ_1 - μ_2, then Eq. 6-16 simplifies to the following:

$$t = \frac{(\bar{x}_1 - \bar{x}_2) - d}{\sqrt{\dfrac{s_1^2}{n_1} + \dfrac{s_2^2}{n_2}}} \qquad \text{(Eq. 6-18)}$$

The-p-values for these types of tests are similar to that shown in Table 6-3. They are modified here to show degrees of freedom specific to this problem type:

Number of Tails	Function
1-Tailed Test	tdist($|t|$, df, 1)
2-Tailed Test	tdist($|t|$, df, 2)

Table 6.8. Functions for p-value.

Let's do an example using the data set "ExamScores." This data set compares the scores from two different exams administered at a public university with very large classes. Exam 1 was taken before Exam 2. We are interested in seeing if the performances on the two exams were the same at the $\alpha = 0.05$ level. We have the following hypotheses:

$$H_0: (\mu_1 - \mu_2) = 0; \quad H_A: (\mu_1 - \mu_2) \neq 0 \qquad \text{(Eq. 6-19)}$$

The following descriptive statistics are captured from the data set:

Quantity	Exam 1	Exam 2
Sample Size	$n_1 = 500$	$n_2 = 500$
Sample Mean	$\bar{x}_1 = 80.00$	$\bar{x}_2 = 77.00$
Sample Standard Deviation	$s_1 = 4.00$	$s_2 = 6.99$

Table 6.9. Summary Data for Difference in Exam Scores

The data set results in $df = 796.23$. Our critical value is obtained via t.inv.2t(0.05, 796.23) = +/- 1.96, and we have a test statistic of t = 8.33. Because the test-statistic is more extreme than the critical value, we reject H_0, and claim that the performances between Exams 1 and 2 were not the same. Our p-value is obtained via Table 6-8, which is tdist(|8.33|, 796.23), which is less than 0.0001.

We will do another example of differences between means. Both Alberto and Guillermo are world-class runners, specializing in the 400m dash. Alberto claims that he averages one second faster in the event than does his competitor Guillermo. Using this information, we can construct the following hypotheses:

$$H_0: (\mu_G - \mu_A) = 1; \; H_A: (\mu_G - \mu_A) \neq 1 \text{[3]} \qquad \text{(Eq. 6-20)}$$

We will use $\alpha = 0.03$. Our data set "Time400m" yields the following statistics:

Quantity	Guillermo	Alberto
Sample Size	$n_G = 13$	$n_A = 15$
Sample Mean	$\bar{x}_G = 45.8s$	$\bar{x}_A = 44.6s$
Sample Standard Deviation	$s_G = 0.23s$	$s_A = 0.18s$

Table 6.10. Summary Data for 400m Times

The degrees of freedom, as determined via Eq. 6-15 is 22.65. Our critical value is t.inv.2t(1 – 0.03, 22.65), which is +/- 2.32. Our test statistic, as determined via Eq. 6-18 is as follows:

---

[3] Here, Guillermo's hypothesized slower time is subtracting Alberto's hypothesized faster time so as to have a positive value of the test statistic, simplifying understanding We are than essentially saying that Guillermo is more than one second slower than Alberto. Also note that our value of $d = 1$, the hypothesized difference in average time.

$$t = \frac{(45.8 - 44.6) - 1}{\sqrt{\dfrac{0.23^2}{13} + \dfrac{0.18^2}{15}}} = 2.53 \qquad \text{(Eq. 6-21)}$$

Given that our test statistic is more extreme than our critical value, we reject H_0 and claim that Alberto is in fact more than one second faster than Guillermo. As stated in the structure of the actual test statistic, Guillermo is more than one second slower than Alberto. The p-value is tdist(2.32, 22.65, 2) = 0.0189.

6.5 Confidence Intervals and Two-Tailed Test

It is possible that you may have noticed some similarities between the two-tailed test and confidence intervals. This would not be a coincidence – there is a definite relationship. When we construct a confidence interval, we are using the estimated value of expectation (such as $\bar{x}$) to form an interval where we are $1 - \alpha$ confident the true population lies. This action is very similar to a two-tailed test. In fact, if we construct a confidence interval using some value of α, and that interval contains the hypothesized population parameter (such as μ), we know that we fail to reject H_0 at that particular value of α. Conversely, if the interval does not contain the population parameter, we know to reject H_0 at that specific value of α.

As an example, let's re-visit our Cheerios example. Using the formulae from Section 5.1 and the Cheerios data set, we construct a 95% confidence that is as follows:

$$P(13.99 \leq \mu \leq 14.08) = 0.95 \qquad \text{(Eq. 6-22)}$$

One will notice that the hypothesized population mean of 14 *is* included in this interval, telling us that H_0 is not to be rejected. Conversely, if the hypothesized population mean was not in this interval, we would reject H_0.

Because of this unique relationship between confidence intervals, and two-tailed tests, we essentially added value to confidence intervals.

6.6 Conclusions

It is my opinion that hypothesis testing is the most difficult part of learning statistics. It is also my belief that it is the most important part of statistics. Making a proclamation to the world requires a formal test so as to support the proclamation – at least this is true in the scientific community, which is an important community in society. As such, it is imperative that we understand hypothesis testing.

While the topic may be difficult, it is not unreasonably difficult. The most important part is to understand and visualize the H_0 and H_A. Once this is accomplished, the rest falls into place. Of course, practice is needed so that the proper formulae and Excel functions are correctly used in the pursuit of the problems.

6.7 Exercises

For problems involving actual hypothesis testing of data, the following steps are required:

a) State the appropriate hypotheses
b) Report the critical value.
c) Report the test statistic
d) State your decision regarding H_0.
e) Report the p-value.

1. Use the criminal justice system in the US to provide an example of a Type I error.
2. Use the criminal justice system in the US to provide an example of a Type II error.
3. Mike Trout of the Anaheim Angels thinks his batting average exceeds 0.320. What are the appropriate hypotheses associated with this claim?
4. Motorola invented the concept of six-sigma – claiming production of less than 3.4 defects per million units produced. What are the appropriate hypotheses associated with this claim?
5. LeBron James claims that when Cleveland plays Chicago in basketball, Cleveland beats them by an average of six points. What are the appropriate hypotheses associated with this claim?
6. Use the "WireGaugeData" set to determine, via hypothesis testing at the $\alpha = 0.05$ level if there is a difference in wire diameter.

7. A courier service advertises that its average delivery time is less than 6 hours for local deliveries. A random sample of times for 12 deliveries to an address across town was recorded. These data are shown below. Is this sufficient evidence to support the courier's advertisement at the 5% level of significance? Delivery time data: 3.03, 6.33, 6.50, 5.22, 3.56, 6.76, 7.98, 4.82, 7.96, 4.54, 5.09, 6.46

8. Mike's Bikes in Columbus, Georgia sells a great many road bikes. One of the things that causes Mike Reynolds (the store's proprietor) heartburn is customers coming back in with tire problems. If too much air is put into the tires, blowouts can occur, which are dangerous. In addition to blowouts, the inner tubes must be replaced, which is difficult. If too little air is put into the tires, poor bike performance results, specifically frequent tire replacement.   Mike is wondering if his mechanics are putting the correct amount of air in the tires. The correct amount of air needed for the tires is 115 psi (pounds of air pressure per square inch). Mike randomly sampled 100 inflated tires, and discovered the mean tire pressure to be 113.58 psi, with a standard deviation of 8.1 psi. At the $\alpha = 0.08$ level, what can we conclude about the tire pressure at Mike's?

9. ThreeGuys Chemical Corporation in Cincinnati has a new sodium nitrate rust inhibitor out. The product (called The MoistureBasher) is marketed as a process additive for machine parts used in high-humidity environments. Three Guys claims that when using the MoistureBasher, machine parts can last for 90 days prior to needing replaced due to rusting. A consumer-advocacy group based in Boston decided to test this claim of ThreeGuys – they believe the rust protection is less than 90 days. They treated 20 machine parts with the MoistureBasher and measured the usable duration of machines parts treated with the product. They found a mean duration of 81 days with a standard deviation of 2.5 days. What does this sample information say about the performance claim of ThreeGuys?

10. Individuals filing Federal Income Tax returns prior to March 31 had an average refund of $1,056. Consider the population of "last minute"

filers who mail their returns during the last five days of the income tax period (April 10-15). A sample of 400 late filers was collected, and it was determined that their average refund was $910 with a standard deviation of $1,600. Do late filers receive a refund less than $1,056? Use $\alpha = 0.05$.

11. Ten years ago, the A.C. Nielson service claimed that on average, an American household watched 6.70 hours of television per day. An independent market research group believes that more television is watched now. To test this claim, 200 households were surveyed, and they found a mean of 7.25 hours of television are watched now, with a standard deviation of 2.5 hours. Has the amount of television viewing increased over the last ten years? Use $\alpha = 0.02$.

12. Historically, evening long-distance phone calls from a particular city average 15.2 minutes per call. In a random sample of 35 calls, the sample mean time was 14.3 minutes per call, with a sample standard deviation of 5 minutes. Use this sample information to test for any change in the mean duration of long-distance phone calls. Use $\alpha = 0.02$.

13. A manufacturer of a nylon rope claims that their 10 mm rope withstands a load of more than 250 pounds of force before breaking. To validate this claim, several ropes were subjected to loads and the force at which they broke was documented. These forces are expressed in pounds, and are as follows: 280, 259, 255, 238, 245, 265, 250, 259, 241 and 260. Use $\alpha = 0.06$. Is the manufactures claim credible?

14. A large manufacturer of an electronic component claims that their 0.5 V connecter is consistently produced at a rate of less than 10 defective units per million units produced. Sampling has revealed that the last several lots had defects per million units produced as follows: 3, 8, 7, 13, 8, 4, 11, 10, 9, 6, 10 and 8. Is the manufacturer's claim of less than 10 defects per million legitimate? Use $\alpha = 0.04$.

15. Use the "DiabeticFoods" data set, and perform the appropriate hypotheses.

16. Use the "FinanceProfessors" data set, and perform the appropriate hypotheses.

17. Use the "NFLLinemen" data set, and perform the appropriate hypotheses.

18. Use the "PulseRate" data set, and perform the appropriate hypotheses.

19. Use the data from Problem 5-4. Do a majority of Oregonians support medicinal marijuana?

20. Use the data from Problem 5-3. Do a majority of North Carolinians consider Wake Forest University the best school on the state?

21. Luca Brazzi wishes for the extra-large pizza pies at his pizzeria to have 15 pepperoni slices each. Too few slices result in unhappy customers, and too many slices reduce the profitability of the operation. Luca has randomly sampled several extra-large pizzas and has recorded the number of pepperoni slices on each pizza. This data is included in the "PepperoniSlices" data set. Is the pizzeria putting the appropriate number of pepperoni slices on the pizza? Use $\alpha = 0.03$.

22. A manufacturer of allergy relief medication claims that they have come up with a pill that provides more than eight hours of allergy relief. Because claims related to the pharmaceutical industry require scrutiny, a value of $\alpha=0.01$ must be used. Several severe allergy sufferers were tested using this medication, and the hours of allergy relief that they gained is reported via the included data set ("AllergyRelief"). Your job is to either validate or refute the pharmaceutical firm's claim.

23. Luca Brazzi's pizzeria also delivers pizza and sandwiches to their Brooklyn-based customers. Luca promises the customers a delivery time of less than thirty minutes. To make sure delivery time is in fact less than 30 minutes, Luca has randomly collected delivery times over the last few months of operation. These data are included in the "PizzaDeliveryTime" data set. Is the delivery time less than 30 minutes? Use $\alpha = 0.06$.

24. The Provost of a prestigious regional college is concerned that freshman students are spending too little time studying. She thinks that freshman students study less than six hours per day. To put this concern to the test, she gathered a small sample of students and asked them to report the hours of study time that they incurred on a single day. The hours of study data are available via the included data set ("StudyTime"). A statistics professor from the mathematics department suggested that the Provost use a value of $\alpha=0.10$ for the test. Your job is to test the veracity of the Provost's claim.

25. The U.S. National Park Service claims that the Old Faithful Geyser in Yellowstone National Park requires an average of 78 minutes between eruptions. To validate this claim, the time between eruptions was measured at random intervals by the U.S. Geological Survey. They measured, in minutes, the time that elapsed from the start of one eruption until the start of the next. These measurement values are available via the attached data set. Use a value of $\alpha = 0.05$. Is Old Faithful that "faithful?"

26. A month or so ago, an angry customer complained to Luca Brazzi that the waiting time for a table was too long. The customer told Luca that the waiting time was in excess of 20 minutes during the dinner rush (between 6 and 8 PM). Luca wanted to investigate the angry customer's claim, so he randomly gathered waiting time data for the dinner rush. This waiting time data is included under the "RestaurantWaitingTime" data set. Is the waiting time in excess of 20 minutes? Use $\alpha = 0.005$.

7. Oneway Analysis of Variance

It is often important for us to determine whether or not means from different populations are similar. In fact, we did this exact thing in Section 6.4. Unfortunately, the tools provided in Section 6.4 restrict us to exploring similarity in means when only two populations are involved. This chapter provides the tools to explore similarity in means from two or more populations.

When determining whether or not populations differ in terms of mean values, it is helpful to define a few new terms. A **factor** is categorical variable, also known as a **treatment**. It can be thought of as a data type. When considering the hypothetical example of determining whether or not defects per million units produced are the same across each shift, the shift can be thought of as a factor. This factor, for this particular example, has three unique **levels**: first, second and third shifts. Using this terminology, we can relate the measured value to the factor. For instance, we can ask the same question in mathematical form as follows:

Defects / Million Units Produced = f(Shift)

This question is asking whether or not defects per million units produced is related to the shift. If defects are related to shift, we can conclude that shift does have an effect on defects. Otherwise, we must conclude that shift does not have an effect on shift.

7.1 Variation and the F-Distribution

To determine whether or not means are the same across multiple populations (there are a populations), we first need to establish the appropriate hypotheses. They are as follows:

$$H_0: \ \mu_1 = \mu_2 = \mu_3 \ ... = \ ... \mu_a \hspace{2cm} \text{(Eq. 7-1)}$$
$$H_A: \ \text{not all means are equal}$$

The reason this tool is called Analysis of Variance ("ANOVA" for short) is because at the heart of our analysis, we are comparing two variations. The F-statistic does this via a ratio of two measures of variation. Before presenting this statistic, we need to define a few terms.

Term	Definition
a	number of groups, or populations
n_i	sample size of group i (i = 1, 2, ..., a)
$\bar{x}_i$	sample mean of group i
s_i	sample standard deviation of group i
x_{it}	the ith observation of group t
$\bar{\bar{x}}$	mean of all sample data

Table 7.1. Terms Used for ANOVA

The values in Table 7.1 are used to determine the F-statistic, which is the ratio of two variation measures. In its most general form, the F-statistic looks like this:

$$F = \frac{Between\ Group\ Variation}{Within\ Group\ Variation} \qquad \text{(Eq. 7-2)}$$

What this statistic tells us is that F measures how much "distance" there is between groups compared to how much variation each group has on its own. If this ratio is large, we can claim that group means are in fact statistically different (reject H_0). Otherwise, we cannot claim a significant difference between groups (fail to reject H_0). In more specific terms, our F-statistic looks like this:

$$F = \frac{\sum_{i=1}^{a} n_i(\bar{x}_i - \bar{\bar{x}})^2/(a-1)}{\sum_{i=1}^{a}\sum_{t=1}^{n_i}(x_{it} - \bar{x}_i)^2/\sum_{i=1}^{a}(n_i - 1)} \qquad \text{(Eq. 7-3)}$$

There is no doubt that the formula above is complicated, and inappropriate for business students to pursue. Fortunately, Microsoft Excel and other software packages calculate this value for us. More on this shortly.

It is appropriate to note that like for other hypothesis tests, a p-value accompanies the F-statistic, and like with other p-values we've pursued, a smaller p-value implies we should reject the H_0.

As an example of the F-statistic and how it determines significant differences in means between groups, we turn to a simple ANOVA example, where there are two groups. Specifically, an issue I deal with when teaching statistics to my MBA students. On Monday evening, I give an exam to my

Working Professional students in Charlotte. On Tuesday evening, I give the same exam to my Working Professional students in Winston-Salem. After grading the exams, I am always interested in seeing whether or not there is a difference in performance between the two classes – I want both classes to both do well, and sometimes I fear that one group is doing better (or worse) than the other. ANOVA is the ideal tool to help me address this question. These examples are presented in the context of the F-statistic, and its associated p-value.

Consider a scenario where the exam score for the Charlotte class is about 86, and the average exam score for the Winston-Salem class is about 85. The standard deviation for both classes is about 5.5. The F-statistic for this scenario is 0.07 (and an associated p-value of 0.7971), with a between group variation of 39.20, and a within group variation of 25.8. Clearly, there is no significant difference between the groups. Figure 7-1 supports this via a combined histogram for the two classes.

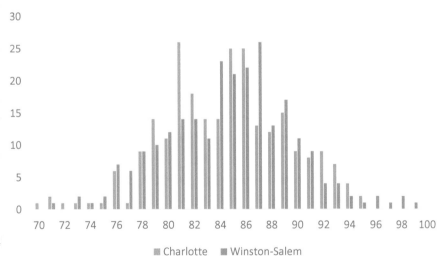

Figure 7.1. No Significant Difference Between Groups.

From a graphical standpoint, Figure 7.1 shows no separation between the two groups. As such, we are unable to claim any differences between the groups.

Now we consider a scenario where the means of the two groups are the same as they were before, but this time, the sample standard deviations are about 4 for each group. This results in an F-statistic of 2.80, with a between group variation of 45.00 and a within group variation of 16.05. The F-statistic has an associated p-value of about 0.0947. Figure 7-2 shows the combined histogram of this scenario.

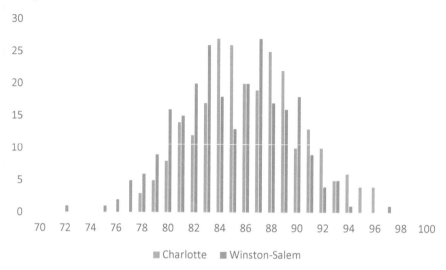

Figure 7-2. Some Significant Difference Between Groups

Here, we may notice that there is some evidence that the Charlotte class has done slightly better than the Winston-Salem class, because there is more "blue" to the right, and more "red" to the right. Nevertheless, our evidence is less than compelling.

As a final example, let us consider once again that Charlotte's average is about 86, while the Winston-Salem average is about 85. This time, however, the standard deviation for both classes is about 1. This gives us an F-statistic of 100.66 (and an associated p-value of < 0.0001), a between group variation of 106.72 and a within group variation of 1.06. Figure 7-3 shows us the results via a combined histogram.

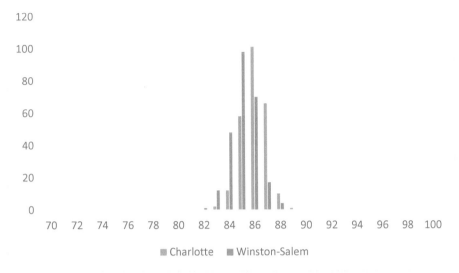

Figure 7.3. Significant Difference Between Groups.

Figure 7.3 shows that there is a definite difference in groups.

The point in showing these three scenarios is to emphasize how the F-statistic controls our decision as to whether or not to reject H_0. In each of these scenarios, the difference in means is about 1 point, implying that the between group variation is essentially the same. But as we proceed through the example, our within group variation decreases, thereby increasing the F-statistic, making us more likely to reject H_0. Difference in means can be small, but if there is consistency within each group, we can still claim significant differences between groups. This is what the F-statistic tells us.

7.2 Testing Equality of Means from Multiple Populations

Fortunately, we do not have to construct H_0 and H_A for ANOVA tests. The reason for this is because the test is the same way every time. H_0 states that all means are equal, while H_A states that not all means are equal. This never changes. As such, software packages always compute the means and standard deviations for each group, and them compute the F-statistic and report the associated p-value.

As an example, consider the Excel data set "ShiftDefectData." For this data set, there is a column for each of three shifts of a factory. Each data value shows the number of defects per million units for the appropriate shift. We are interested in knowing if defects per million are the same for each shift. This is very straightforward in Microsoft Excel. We need to have an Excel data set with a unique column for each unique population – in this case, each population is a shift. We use the Data Analysis tools and select "ANOVA: Single Factor." From there, we select the data we wish to use for analysis. Again, each column represents a unique population. We indicate whether or not our data set has column headings, we input our level of significance (α = 0.05) is the default. We then select our desired output range then select OK. We are given the ANOVA output, which is summarized in Table 7-2.

Groups	Count	Sum	Average	Variance
Shift 1	62	3033	48.92	219.42
Shift 2	62	2733	44.08	174.08
Shift 3	62	2913	46.98	258.80

Variation Source	SS	df	MS	F	P-val
Between Groups	735.48	2	367.74	1.69	0.1871
Within Groups	39790	183	217.43		
Total	40526	185			

Table 7-2. ANOVA Output for Defects by Shift Problem

The first part of Figure 7-2 shows the descriptive statistics for each of the three shifts. The average number of defects per shift is of greatest interest to us. You will notice that the defects per million for the three shifts ranges from around 44 to about 49. The ANOVA table below shows the F-statistic (F = 1.69) and its associated p-value. You will see that the p-value is high (0.1871), which prevents us from saying the defects per million units made are essentially the same for each shift. Because of this, I am reluctant to present a combined histogram of defects/million for each shift, as we'd be unable to show any distinction between the histograms. For this problem, we can conclude that shift *does not* have an effect on defects. Incidentally, the remainder of the

ANOVA table simply shows the derivation of the F-statistic.

As another example, let us look at the useful life of tools coated with three different metals: nickel, phosphorus and zinc. We wish to study the useful tool life for each group of tools.

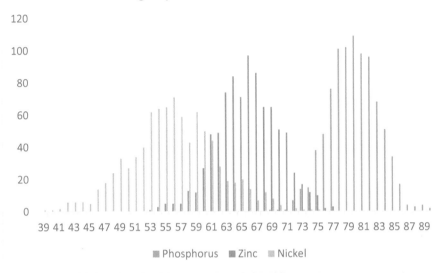

Figure 7-4. Useful Tool Life by Metal Treatment

From the combined histogram in Figure 7.4, it appears that phosphorus gives us the longest tool life, followed by zinc, with nickel providing us with the shortest tool life. However, we cannot make this statement in any official capacity until we perform the appropriate ANOVA test. Using Excel in a similar fashion to the last example, we have the following ANOVA output, as shown in Table 7.3.

Groups	Count	Sum	Average	Variance
Phosphorus	890	71090	79.88	10.30
Zinc	878	57864	65.90	16.38
Nickel	872	48867	56.04	33.30

Variation Source	SS	df	MS	F	P-val
Between Groups	253026	2	126513	6352.38	0^4
Within Groups	52518	2637	20		
Total	305544	2639			

Table7.3. ANOVA Output for Tool Life by Metal Treatment Problem

As one can see from Figures 7.4 and Table7.3, there is strong evidence for us to claim that the three metal treatments do not result in similar useful tool lives, with F = 6352.38 and a corresponding p-value < 0.0001. Despite the p-value showing "0" above, we can never claim a p-value equal to 0, so we say that is it < 0.0001. The reason for this is that we are using sample data from a larger population, and the p-value will always have value in excess of 0. For this problem, we can conclude that the metal treatment *does have* an effect on tool life.

7.3 Multiple Factor Analysis of Variance

In this chapter, we have pursued ANOVA via a single factor only. There are situations where multiple factors might also be considered. For example, what if we were interested in studying whether or not both the gender of the salesperson and the day of the week have an effect on car sales. We could pose this question mathematically:

Car Sales = f(Gender of Salesperson, Day of Week)

This question has two factors (Gender and Day), where Gender has two levels (Male and Female), and Day of Week has seven levels (each day of the week). We can pursue these types of questions via Multiple Factor ANOVA. Unfortunately, adding factors to ANOVA problems complicates the problem

---

[4] Excel displays the p-value here as "0," but it should be "< 0.0001." Excel does this when confronted with p-values less than 10^{-128}.

to a very large degree. As such, it is left to more specialized books for coverage of multiple factor ANOVA.

7.4 Conclusions

ANOVA determines whether or not some factor has an effect on the value of some other variable. This factor can be considered a categorical variable – a variable we cannot precisely measure numerically. Certainly we can assign a number to a shift, but this is only a relative to other shifts. We cannot measure specific metal treatments, gender of a salesperson or a specific day of the week. Nevertheless, we are exploring a possible relationship between a categorical variable and a numerical variable. When we get to the chapter on Simple Linear Regression, our categorical variable will be replaced with a numerical variable. Because of this, there is a strong relationship between Single-Factor ANOVA and Simple Linear Regression. Chapter 9 will pursue this further.

7.5 Exercises

1. I am interested in pursuing the relationship between temperature and the time of day. What is the categorical variable, and what is the numerical variable? How many levels does the categorical variable have?

2. Use the "GenderSalesData" file for this problem. At the $\alpha = 0.05$ level, does Gender have an effect on sales volume? Report the mean sales for each Gender and justify your response accordingly.

3. Use the "GenderSalesData" file for this problem. At the $\alpha = 0.07$ level, does Day of the week have an effect on sales volume? Report the mean sales for each Day and justify your response accordingly.

4. Use the "ServerComplaints" data file for this problem. At the $\alpha = 0.03$ level, does server have an effect on the percent of restaurant customers who complain about the service? Report the mean complaint percentage for each server and justify your response accordingly.

5. Use the "ExamDay" data file for this problem. Professor Fraud teaches statistics on Monday, Wednesday and Friday. When he gives his

students an exam, it will be on one of these days. The data set shows randomly selected exam scores for students taking exams on these days. At the $\alpha = 0.05$ level, does the day of the exam have an effect on the exam score? Present the means for the exam days, and use this to justify your result.

6. Use the "WhisperingPines" data set for this question. Arnold, Jack and Tiger are reputable golfers, and Whispering Pines is a famous golf course, with a rich history. There are four Par 5s on the golf course. On a par 5, a professional golfer is expected to get their ball on the green in three shots. However, the best golfers try to get their ball on the green in two shots, so as to increase their probability for a good score. If a golfer gets their ball on the green of a par 5 in two shots, they have been successful at this challenge. The data set includes randomly-selected success rates for Arnold, Jack and Tiger for some of their rounds of golf played at par 5 holes at the Whispering Pines golf course. Using $\alpha = 0.03$, are the success rates unique for the three golfers?

7. As a follow-up to the previous question, is Tiger's success rate unique from that of the other two golfers? Again, use $\alpha = 0.03$.

8. For this question, use the "HousePricesFourCities" data set. There are four cities involved here: Indianapolis, Boston, Rochester and San Diego. For each city, randomly-selected real-estate transaction prices have been shown. At the $\alpha = 0.01$ level, can we say that the city has an effect on the transaction price?

9. Using the same data set as above, and $\alpha = 0.01$, can we claim a difference in transaction price between San Diego and Boston?

8. Chi-Square Testing

In our study of statistics, there are often times when we are given a distribution of data and we need to "tell the world" the type of data distribution we have. One way to do this is by inspection. For example, if our histogram shows a peak in the middle of the data, the histogram is symmetric, and low frequencies of outcomes lie in the tails, a normal distribution is a good guess. Unfortunately, it is not always that easy.

Because of these inherent difficulties, we sometimes need to perform a formal test to determine if a given (observed) data distribution fits that of a theoretical (expected) data distribution. In order to do this, we perform a chi-square test.

In this chapter, we will cover two types of chi-square tests. The first is called a "goodness of fit" test to see if a given data distribution matches that of an expected distribution. The second type of test is called a "test of independence," where we determine if the variables associated with a marginal probability table are independent of each other.

8.1 The Chi-Square Test

The formal test to determine if an observed distribution matches a theoretical data distribution is a chi-square test. The appropriate hypotheses are as follows

H_0: the given distribution fits the expected distribution   (Eq. 8-1)

H_A: the given distribution does not fit the expected distribution

As is the case with ANOVA, these hypotheses are always the case, and the need to formally state these hypotheses is not as necessary as it is for the tests we performed in Chapter 6.

The chi-square distribution is the tool we use to address the hypotheses presented above. This distribution formally tests whether or not there is equality in two sets of outcomes. Of course, for our purposes, one set of outcomes is the observed distribution and the other set of outcomes is the expected distribution. With this stated, assuming we have n possible outcomes, we compare the observed frequencies (f_o) with the expected frequencies, and derive our chi-square test-statistic as follows:

$$\chi^2 = \sum_{i=1}^{n} \left(\frac{\left(f_{o(i)} - f_{e(i)} \right)^2}{f_{e(i)}} \right)$$

(Eq. 8-2)

This statistic takes the squared difference between the observed and expected frequencies for each outcome and then divides by the expected frequency for standardization purposes. The summation accounts for all possible outcomes. If this value exceeds some critical value, we reject H_0 and claim a difference between observed and expected distributions. Table 8-1 shows the critical value and p-values associated with a chi-square test for a level of significance = α and n possible outcomes.

Function	Definition
chiinv(α, n-1)	critical value of a chi-square test
chidist(χ^2, n-1)	p-value of a chi-square test

Table 8-1. Excel Functions for Chi-Square Test

8.2 Goodness of Fit Test

The simplest type of chi-square test is to see whether or not a given set of observed data fits an expected distribution, which, as we stated earlier, is called a "goodness of fit" test.

A good example of this is to roll a single die 100 times and study the frequency of the six possible outcomes. Given that we expect each outcome to occur with a 1/6 probability, each outcome over 100 trials will be 100/6, which is 16.66. Table 8-2 shows the observed frequencies, compared to the expected frequencies when 100 rolls were simulated. The table also shows the by-outcome detail of the chi-square statistic shown in Eq. 8-2.

Outcome	1	2	3	4	5	6
Observed	21	13	9	21	17	19
Expected	16.67	16.67	16.67	16.67	16.67	16.67
$(f_o-f_e)^2/f_e$	1.13	0.81	3.53	1.13	0.01	0.33

Table 8-2. Chi-Square Test for Single Die Roll

When we sum the bottom row of this table, we have a χ^2 statistic of 6.92.

Using a $\alpha = 0.05$ level of significance, we have a critical value of 11.07. Because our χ^2 test statistic of 6.92 does not exceed our critical value of 110.07, we cannot reject the H_0. As such, we conclude the observed distribution is the same as the given distribution, with a p-value of 0.2267. In layman's terms, we can claim the single die "is fair." Figure 8-1 below shows the results via a histogram – notice the small difference in the height of each bar.

Figure 8-1. Histogram of Die Roll

We can also test a data set of observed data to see if they follow a normal distribution. We learned in Chapter 4 that a normal distribution is a continuous distribution (one with infinite possible outcomes), which doesn't coordinate well with the discrete nature of chi-square testing. Nevertheless, we can use the "norm.dist" function in Excel to transform the continuous nature of a normal distribution to one with a discrete nature. The "norm.dist" function takes on the following form:

$$f(x_i) = \text{norm.dist}(\mu, \sigma, x_i, \text{false})$$ (Eq. 8-3)

This function returns the normal density function associated with the given arguments: μ is the hypothesized population mean; σ is the standard deviation of the normal distribution; x_i is a specific outcome, and "false" request the density function value associated with these arguments, as opposed to the cumulative density function. We can convert this density function to a probability – specifically the probability of outcome i occurring as follows:

$$P(x_i) = \frac{norm.\,dist(\mu, \sigma, x_i, false)}{\sum_{i=1}^{n} norm.\,dist(\mu, \sigma, x_i, false)} \quad \text{(Eq. 8-4)}$$

This is an approximation for the probability of some specific outcome i occurring. We can convert this approximated probability into an expected frequency value $(f_{e(i)})$ via the following, where m is the number of observations in the data set:

$$f_{e(i)} = mP(x_i) \quad \text{(Eq. 8-5)}$$

At this point, we are able to conduct our chi-square test because we have values of f_o and f_e for all possible outcomes.

Let us illustrate chi-square testing for a normal distribution via an example. Let us suppose that a company makes medication in 20mg tablets. The company claims variation on the size of the tablets, but says they have a mean mass of 20mg, with a standard deviation of 0.25mg. The company's quality control department randomly selected 361 tablets and measured their mass to the nearest 0.1mg. These possible outcomes and observed frequencies (f_o) are shown in the first two columns of Table 8-3. Given that we have f_o values, we direct our attention to finding f_e values. We start with Eq. 8-3 and 8-4 to compute first normal density values and then convert them to probabilities. These values are shown in the third and fourth columns of Table 8-3. We then convert the probabilities of the various outcomes by multiplying the probabilities by $m = 361$ total observations. This results in our expected frequencies (f_e) shown in the fifth column of Table 8-3. From here, we can calculate our χ^2 statistic, which the sixth column of Table 8-3 shows us to be 24.07. Using the "chidist" function, we learn that this test has a p-value of 0.0639. As such, for any value of α that is less than 0.0639, we can claim that the mass of the tablets are normally distributed.

Outcome	f_o	$f(x_i)$	$P(x_i)$	f_e	$(f_o-f_e)^2/f_e$
19.4	6	0.09	0.01	3.25	2.33
19.5	6	0.22	0.02	7.83	0.43
19.6	18	0.44	0.04	16.09	0.23
19.7	37	0.78	0.08	28.17	2.77
19.8	49	1.16	0.12	42.02	1.16
19.9	48	1.47	0.15	53.42	0.55
20.0	56	1.60	0.16	57.87	0.06
20.1	38	1.47	0.15	53.42	4.45
20.2	41	1.16	0.12	42.02	0.02
20.3	29	0.78	0.08	28.17	0.02
20.4	20	0.44	0.04	16.09	0.95
20.5	8	0.22	0.02	7.83	0.00
20.6	2	0.09	0.01	3.25	0.48
20.7	1	0.03	0.00	1.15	0.02
20.8	1	0.01	0.00	0.35	1.24
20.9	1	0.00	0.00	0.09	9.36
Sum	361	9.96	1		24.07

Table 8.3. Calculations for Normality Test

Figure 8-2 shows a combined histogram for Chi-Square test for normality.

Normal Distribution Chi-Square Test

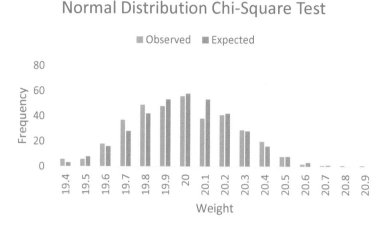

Figure 8-2. Chi-Square Test for Normality

We can also test whether or not some given distribution is binomial. This is easier than testing for normality, because the binomial distribution is discrete by nature, and making an approximation from continuous to discrete is not needed here. Given a data set of observed frequencies (f_o), we can estimate the probability of success (p), and then use the binomial distribution to determine f_e values for our chi-square test.

Consider an example of a semi-retired doctor who practices medicine in a rural area. He has five appointments per day. At the end of the day, the office manager maintains a tally of patients seen on time. For example, if there is a certain day where the doctor sees two patients on time, the tally for two patients seen on time is incremented by one. Table 8.4 shows the last 100 days of on-time performance:

On-Time	0	1	2	3	4	5
Frequency (f_o)	22	26	34	11	5	2

Table 8.4. Summary of Patients Seen On-Time

We would like to know if this data follows a binomial distribution. Since we are not given the probability of success for a patient being seen on-time, we need to estimate this value. We can do this by first determining the number of patients seen on time: 0(22) + 1(26) + 2(34) + 3(11) + 4(5) + 5(2), which is 157. Since there was 500 total patients seen (5 patients/day over 100 days), the probability of a patient being seen on time is 157 / 500, which is 0.314. This value is used in the "binom.dist" function, which will provide us with probabilities associated with the number of "successes" from 0 to 5 patients being seen on time. For a reminder of the binom.dist function, please refer to Section 4.1.2. Using this function, along with multiplying each of these binomial probabilities by 100 days, we have the following:

Successes	0	1	2	3	4	5
f_o	22	26	34	11	5	2
Binomial Prob.	0.15	0.35	0.32	0.15	0.03	0.00
f_e	15.19	34.77	31.83	14.57	3.33	0.31
$(f_e\text{-}f_o)^2/f_e$	3.05	2.21	0.15	0.87	0.83	9.41

Table 8.5. Chi-Square Test Results for On-Time Visits

The values in the bottom row of Table 8.5 result in a χ^2 statistic of 16.53, with an associated p-value of 0.0055. At any credible value of α, we would reject H_0, and claim that the binomial distribution does not describe the given data set. Figure 8.3 shows the non-matching histograms, supporting our decision to reject H_0.

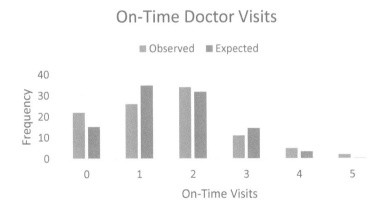

Figure 8.3. Chi-Square Test for On-Time Doctor Visits

8.3 Test for Independence

When performing goodness of fit tests, we are essentially comparing an observed set of outcomes with an expected set of outcomes. We can take this mindset further and explore whether or not multiple entities are related. What is meant by this is that we can determine whether or not multiple seemingly unrelated entities are in fact related. We can use our chi-square test approach to explore this – we call this a test for independence. In the context of H_0 and H_A, we state the following:

H_0: Multiple entities are independent of each other   (Eq. 8-6)
H_A: Multiple entities are dependent on each other

To explore what we can do for a test of independence, let us re-visit Table 3.1, where we have a breakdown of voting on a congressional bill by political party. Voting details have been omitted, and only row and column totals are shown, along with percentages

	Yes	No	Total
Republican			242 (56.94%)
Democrat			183 (43.06%)
Total	275 (64.71%)	150 (35.29%)	425

Table 8.6. House Vote Template on HR 1599

Because I know that 64.71% voted "Yes," and 56.94% are Republicans, I *expect* that (64.71%*56.94%*425) 156.59 of the 425 voters are Republicans that voted "Yes."

Formally, this expected frequency value is as follows:

$$f_{e_{(ij)}} = m \left(\frac{\sum row_i}{m} \right) \left(\frac{\sum col_j}{m} \right) \qquad \text{(Eq. 8-7)}$$

Using Eq. 8-7, we can compute the remaining values of Table 8.6 as follows:

	Yes	No
Republican	156.59	85.41
Democrat	118.41	64.59

Table 8.7. "Expected" House Vote on HR 1599

The values in the four "filled" cells of Table 8.7 are based on expectation only – they are independent of political party and/or the actual vote – expected values. The observed values (f_o) are the original values from Table 3.1

	Yes	No
Republican	230	12
Democrat	45	138

Table 8.8. "Observed" House Vote on HR 1599

Revising our formula from Eq 8-2 to determine the test statistic for a chi-square test for independence, we have the following:

$$\chi^2 = \sum_{i=1}^{rows} \sum_{j=1}^{cols} \frac{\left(f_{o(ij)} - f_{e(ij)}\right)^2}{f_{e(ij)}}$$ (Eq. 8-8)

Using Eq. 8-8, we have the following values that need to be summed:

	Yes	No
Republican	34.42	63.10
Democrat	45.51	83.44

Table 8.9. χ^2 Calculation for House Vote on HR 1599

These values sum to 226.47. A chi-square test for independence has degrees of freedom determined as follows:

$$df = (rows - 1)(columns - 1)$$ (Eq. 8-9)

Our test, then, as (2 - 1)(2 - 1) = 1 degree of freedom. This yields a p-value < 0.0001, strongly suggesting that our two entities are not independent of each other. In other words, political party and the actual vote are related to each other, which given our political climate of strong partisanship, this should not be a surprise.

As another example, let's consider a survey completed by university students. These students were asked a question about how optimistic they are about the future. There are three possible responses: Optimistic; Indifferent; and Pessimistic. The survey respondents are also grouped according to class: freshman; sophomore; junior and senior. The observed data ($f_{o(ij)}$) are as follows:

	Fresh.	Soph.	Jr	Sr	Sum
Optimistic	7	3	2	8	20
Indifferent	6	8	9	7	30
Pessimistic	15	15	14	6	50
Sum	28	26	25	21	100

Table 8.10. Observed Frequencies for Example

The expected values are as follows:

	Fresh.	Soph.	Jr.	Sr.	Sum
Optimistic	5.60	5.20	5.00	4.20	20
Indifferent	8.40	7.80	7.50	6.30	30
Pessimistic	14.00	13.00	12.50	10.50	50
Sum	28	26	25	21	100

Table 8.11. Expected Frequencies for Example

Table 8-12 shows the components of the chi-square test statistic for independence.

	Fresh.	Soph.	Jr.	Sr
Optimistic	0.35	0.93	1.80	3.44
Indifferent	0.69	0.01	0.30	0.08
Pessimistic	0.07	0.31	0.18	1.93

Table 8.12. χ^2 Statistic Details for Example Problem

The χ^2 test statistic sums to 10.08. This test has $(3 - 1)(4 - 1) = 6$ degrees of freedom, resulting in a p-value of 0.1215. As such we fail to reject the H_0 and we claim that the entities of the student's opinion and class are independent – they are not related.

8.4 Conclusions

The chi-square test is a powerful, yet simple statistical test. Because of its simplicity, it can be used to make a variety of general determinations. The general intent of this test is to compare the observed data we are provided to the outcomes we expect. When we do this, we can address many important issues of a statistical nature.

In the next chapter, we cover simple linear regression – one of the more important concepts in statistics. With careful data preparation, we can replace regression hypothesis testing with a chi-square test. The motivation to do this is to simplify the process. This is only mentioned as an example of the value of the chi-square test. The power of the chi-square test is its simplicity.

Because of its simplicity and versatility, the chi-square test has the drawback of being somewhat unstructured. Because of this, we sometimes need to conceptualize how we will relate the observed frequencies to the expected frequencies.

8.5 Exercises

1. I flip a coin 103 times, and tails is the result 57 times. At the α = 0.05 level, is the coin fair?
2. I roll a pair of dice 1000 times, and the following outcomes result. At the α = 0.05 level, are the dice fair?

Outcome	2	3	4	5	6
Freq.	25	56	83	112	145

Outcome	7	8	9	10	11	12
Freq.	172	136	108	86	51	26

Use the following data for Problems 3 – 7. I flip a coin 10 times, and I tally the number times I end up with tails. I repeat this experiment 1,000 times, and end up with the following frequency for tails.

Tails	0	1	2	3	4	5
Freq.	1	5	47	115	207	248

Tails	5	6	7	8	9	10
Freq.	248	202	120	41	12	2

3. At the α = 0.05 level, does the data reflect a binomial distribution?
4. At the α = 0.05 level, does the data reflect a normal distribution?

5. At the α = 0.05 level, can we claim a binomial distribution with a probability of tails being 0.5?
6. At the α = 0.05 level, can we claim a normal distribution with an expected value of 5 and a standard deviation of 1.5811?
7. At the α = 0.05, is the coin fair?
8. Consider a company that manufactures lawn mowers. They make the same amount of mowers each day. At the completion of the manufacturing the mowers, the Quality Control department make a final inspection. Below is the average number of daily rejects over the past year.

Day	Mon	Tue	Wed	Thu	Fri
Rejects	21	25	19	22	31

At the α = 0.04 level, are the number of daily reject as expected?

9. Consider a large university with seven colleges. Each year, the number of cheating cases for each college are published by the university. The relevant data is as follows:

School	Cheating Cases	Enrollment
Architecture	6	1,500
Business	51	6,000
Engineering	11	6,000
Liberal Arts	6	1,500
Social Sciences	10	4,000
Sciences	15	4,000
Veterinary Medicine	1	1,000

At the α = 0.05 level, are cheating cases representative of enrollment by college?

10. People were randomly selected across the US to ask if they would like to see gun laws made more restrictive. Specifically, the question was "would you like to see gun laws in the US made more restrictive?" Both men and women were asked the question and the results are below:

	Yes	No
Men	74	51
Women	80	32

Using α = 0.03, are gender and the response to the question independent?

11. Several Americans were randomly selected and asked if they approved of the US Supreme Court's decision to permit same-sex marriage. The respondents were broken into political party affiliation. The data is shown below:

	Democrat	Unafflilated	Republican
Approve	96	31	41
Indifferent	41	42	56
Disapprove	12	38	107

Using α = 0.06, are party affiliation and the approval to same-sex marriage independent?

9. Simple Linear Regression

We have covered the basic foundations of statistical inference — testing a claim via a formal test, so that we can properly articulate our findings to the skeptical scientific community. This is an important accomplishment. This chapter will build on our ability to do this via exploring potential relationships between variables. We read about exploration between variables in everyday life. For example, we have learned about a relationship between exposure to asbestos and mesothelioma, a type of lung cancer. We have learned about a relationship between the amount of time a child watches television and the likelihood of that child being obsese.

These "relationships" are typically implied using very subtle language. Nevertheless, these relationships are almost always determined via some form of linear regression — formally exploring the relationships between variables, or entities. In this chapter, we will cover simple linear regression, which is the exploration between two variables. Many informative and important investigations can be made with just a basic understanding of this powerful tool.

9.1 Slope and Intercept

Prior to delving into regression from a statistical standpoint, it is important for us to recall from high school algebra the formula for a line. The lines has two major components: an **intercept** and a **slope**. The reference system for a line is the Cartesian Coordinate System, where "x" represents the horizontal axis and "y" represents the vertical axis. A point in this coordinate system is represented via "(x, y)" notation. The line has the general formula:

$$y = a + bx \qquad \text{(Eq. 9-1)}$$

Under this scenario, we assume the x-value is pre-determined — we call "x" an **independent variable**. We assume that y-values are determined by the x values — we call "y" a **dependent variable**.

The intercept, represented by "a" is the value of the y-value when "x" equals zero. Graphically, this is where the line crosses the vertical axis (y-axis). The slope, represented by "b" is the ratio of the change in y to each unit change in x. Mathematically, this is often stated as follows:

$$b = \Delta y / \Delta x \qquad \text{(Eq. 9-2)}$$

Figure 9.1 shows a line of the form "$y = 3 + 2x$.

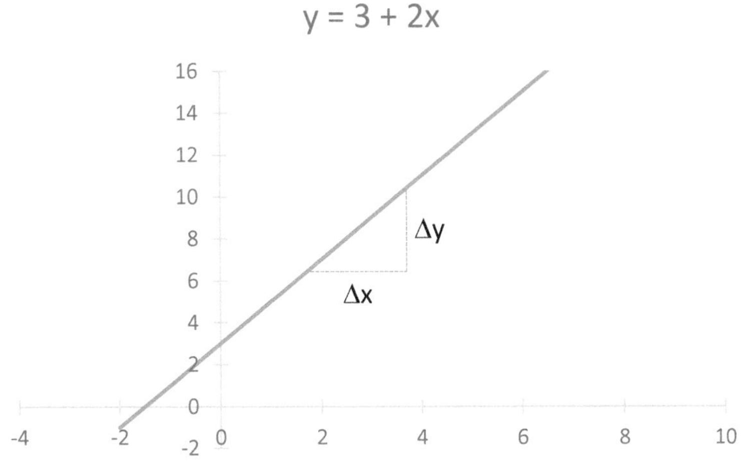

Figure 9.1. Example Linear Model

This example line has an intercept of "3" – notice how the line crosses the vertical axis at $y = 3$ ($y = 3 + 2(0) = 3$). This example line has a slope of "2." The $\Delta y / \Delta x$ ratio is equal to "2" – this is detailed in the "wedged" section of Figure 9.1.

9.2 Ordinary Least Squares Regression

In statistics, we are given a set of data and it is our job to "fit" a line through the points represented by the data set. As an example of a data set, consider a situation where we are interested in exploring the relationship between price and demand of a product. In this example, we have randomly visited convenience stores in Winston-Salem, NC. In each store, we looked at the price of a 12-pack of Diet Dr. Pepper in cans. Management provided us with the sales data for this product in units sold for the previous week. This data set is as follows:

Pr.	3.38	3.42	3.48	3.52	3.55	3.55	3.61	3.61	3.67	3.72
Dem	83	86	83	81	81	83	81	81	80	80

Table 9.1. Price vs. Demand Data for Diet Dr. Pepper

A scatter plot is shown in Figure 9.2.

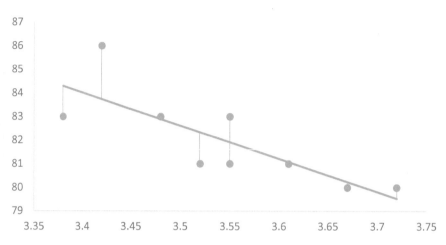

Figure 9.2. Scatter Plot for Diet Dr. Pepper Demand Data

Here we see points, showing the demand for each price, as the result of our random sampling effort. As one might expect, there seems to be an inverse relationship between price and demand – as price increases, demand seems to increase.

In order to find the "best" line relating price to demand, we select a slope and intercept that minimizes the **sum of squared errors**. Figure 9.2 also shows a fitted line. This fitted line is the result of selecting a slope and intercept that minimizes the total squared difference between the actual data points and the fitted line. These error terms are shown via the thin vertical lines spanning the fitted line and the actual data values. We square these error terms for two reasons: first, to prevent negative numbers; second, to amplify large errors. Statistical software will provide us with a slope and intercept value that minimizes the sum of squared errors. The practice of finding the slope and intercept terms is called "**ordinary least squares regression**."

The next section will detail how to perform ordinary least squares regression in Microsoft Excel, but for our data set, we have a slope of -$14.13 and an intercept of 132.05 units of Diet Dr. Pepper. What this means is that when the price is zero, we can expect a demand of 132.05 units. This result, of course, should not be taken literally, but the intercept is where the line crosses the vertical ("y") axis. The slope tells is that for each $1 increase in the price, we can expect demand to *decrease* 14.13 units. The negative sign tells us it is a decrease.

9.3 Statistical Inference for Slope and Intercept

Here, we continue with our Diet Dr. Pepper example and learn how to use Excel to give us the slope and intercept. Then we test the statistical significance of the slope and intercept.

9.3.1 Excel for Regression

In order to learn the values of the slope and intercept, we use the Data Analysis Tools | Regression option. We enter the data associated with the "x" and "y" values. Again, for our example, Price is the "x" variable, and Demand is the "y" variable. We specify an output range and then "run the regression." We get a very comprehensive output report. Selected output is shown in Table 9.2.

	Coefficients	Standard Error	t Stat	P-value
Intercept	142.05	12.87	10.26	< 0.0001
Price	14.13	3.62	-3.90	0.0045

Table 9.2. Slope and Intercept for Diet Dr. Pepper Data Set

The table shows the slope and intercept values that we learned earlier. The other presented data is discussed next.

9.3.2 Testing the Slope and Intercept

Now that we know the values of the slope and intercept, we need to address the question as to whether or not they are statistically significant. To do this, we first present the linear model relating "x" and "y" for an entire population:

$$Y = \alpha + \beta X \tag{Eq. 9-3}$$

Here, the "x" and "y" terms are capitalized to imply data from the entire population. This equation shows "α," which represents the intercept for the population[5], while "β" represents the slope for the population. We need to test the slope and intercept for statistical significance. These hypotheses are as follows:

$$\text{H}_0\text{: } \alpha = 0; \text{ H}_A\text{: } \alpha \neq 0 \tag{Eq. 9-4}$$

$$\text{H}_0\text{: } \beta = 0; \text{ H}_A\text{: } \beta \neq 0 \tag{Eq. 9-5}$$

Eq. 9-4 is a test for the significance of the intercept, while Eq. 9-5 is a test for the significance of the slope. The test for the intercept is not of importance here – the intercept is important in terms of minimizing the sum of squared error value, but for this book, the statistical significance of the intercept is not a matter of concern. What is important, however, is the test for the statistical significance of the slope. In Eq. 9-5, the H_0 states that the slope is equal to zero. This means that as X changes, Y does not change – Y is not sensitive to X. The H_A says that the slope is not equal to zero, meaning that as X changes, Y changes as well – Y is sensitive to X.

These tests for the significance of the slope and intercept are always as presented in these two equations. They are always two-tailed tests. Because of this consistency, we never have to formally state them – they are always the same. This provides Excel, or whatever software is being used to present us the appropriate statistics to interpret. We have to, of course, compare these hypothesized values to the estimated values, which we know to be "a" for the intercept and "b" for the slope. The test statistic for the intercept is as follows:

$$t = \frac{a - \alpha}{se_a} = \frac{a - 0}{se_a} = \frac{a}{se_a} \tag{Eq. 9-6}$$

The test statistic for the slope is as follows:

---

[5] Not to be confused with the level of significance as covered previously. These two entities are independent from each other.

$$t = \frac{b - \beta}{se_b} = \frac{b - 0}{se_b} = \frac{b}{se_b} \qquad \text{(Eq. 9-7)}$$

Because both α and β are hypothesized to be zero, we substitute zero into both equations above, and we end up with the "estimates" of the intercept (a) and slope (b) divided by their standard errors. The end result is the two t-statistics above very closely resemble the t-statistics we used in Chapter 6.

The results of these two-tailed tests are also shown in Table 9.2. When the estimates of the slope and intercept are divided by their standard errors, we have the appropriate t-statistics and p-values. You will notice that the p-value associated with the intercept is < 0.0001. Here, we reject the H_0, and claim the intercept is statistically significant. The t-statistic associated with the slope term is -3.90, with an associated p-value of 0.0045. This tells us that the relationship between Demand and Price is statistically significant – there is a meaningful relationship between price and demand.

9.4 Estimation / Prediction

Let's continue with our Diet Dr. Pepper example and assume that we are satisfied with the belief that Price and Demand have a statistically significant relationship. We can then use the following equation to estimate Demand given some pre-specified or pre-determined Price:

$$\text{Demand} = 132.05 - 14.13 \text{ (Price)} \qquad \text{(Eq. 9-8)}$$

Given this relationship, however, we need to be careful of the values of Price we use to estimate demand. This model was constructed using a minimum Price of $3.38 and a maximum value of $3.72. Because of this, we can only use this model to estimate Demand for values of price in this interval. If we fail to do this, we are, in essence, "extrapolating," which is a pretentious term for "guessing." As such, we should only estimate for values of "x" that are between x_{min} and x_{max}.

There is one other statistic worth discussing, which is the R^2 value. The value of R^2 tells us the percent of variation in our "y" variable that is explained by our "x" variable. This measure of R^2 is essentially a measure of the model's predictive ability. The R^2 value can be as low as zero, and as high as one. We want our R^2 value to be as high as possible, as that would maximize the percent variation in "y" that is explained by "x." For our example problem, the R^2 value is 0.6553. This value is also included with our Excel output. This means that 65.53% of the variation in Demand is explained by Price. This implies, then, that 34.47% of the variation in Demand has not been explained. As such, when using this model for prediction purposes, we should temper our expectations on the quality of our predictive ability, because much of the variation in demand is explained by entities other than price.

9.5 Conclusions

As stated at the beginning of this chapter, linear regression is the study of relationships among variables. This means that our paramount interest is to see if two variables are related. If they are related – meaning we reject the H_0 regarding a slope of zero – then, and one then, can we pursue the topic of prediction. In short, significance is more important than prediction.

With multiple linear regression – using multiple independent variables ("x" variables), we have the ability to increase our predictive ability via increasing the R^2 value associated with a model.

For now, however, it is most important to understand that simple linear regression is mainly concerned about whether or not variables are related, while multiple linear regression is most concerned about optimizing the predictive ability of our model.

9.6 Exercises

1. Earlier in this chapter, while talking about the Diet Dr. Pepper example, I mentioned that if we increased the sample size, we would decrease the p-value associated with the slope term. Why is this the case?

2. Let us revisit the "ExamScores" data set that we used in Chapter 2. This data set has two columns: the "Exam 1" column is the Exam 1 score for a specific student. The "Exam 2" column is the Exam 2 score for the same student. Explain how simple linear regression could be used as a tool to study the student's propensity for success.

3. Using the "ExamScores" data set, are Exam 1 scores and Exam 2 scores related?

4. Using the "ExamScores" data set, report the R^2 term with the Exam 1 score as the independent variable and the Exam 2 score as the dependent variable.

5. Using the "ExamScores" data set, report the R^2 term with the Exam 2 score as the independent variable and the Exam 1 score as the dependent variable.

6. How do you reconcile your results from the above two questions?

7. Using the "ExamScores" data set, what score would you expect a student to get on Exam 2 if they got an 83 on Exam 1?

8. Using the "NewspaperAdvertisements" data set, report on the relationship between Ads/Month and Customers/Month. Is the relationship meaningful?

9. Using the "NewspaperAdvertisements" data set, estimate customers visiting the store per month when 15 advertisements were made for a specific month. Are you comfortable with this estimate? Why or why not?

10. Using the "NewspaperAdvertisements" data set, estimate customers visiting the store per month when 23 advertisements were made for a specific month. Are you comfortable with this estimate? Why or why not?

11. Using the "NewspaperAdvertisements" data set, what is the predictive ability of this model?

12. Using the "BaseballSalaries2014" data set, report on the relationship between the team payroll and winning percentage. Is the relationship meaningful? Do these results surprise you? Why or why not?

13. Using the "BaseballSalaries2014" data set, estimate a team's winning percentage with an annual payroll of $150M. Are you comfortable with this estimate? Why or why not?

14. Using the "BaseballSalaries2014" data set, estimate a team's winning percentage with an annual payroll of $300M. Are you comfortable with this estimate? Why or why not?

15. Using the "BaseballSalaries2014" data set, describe the predictive ability of your model.

16. Look at the two regression plots below. For each plot, the ordinary least squares regression line is fitted through the data. Of the two plots, which one has the higher R² value. Justify your response.

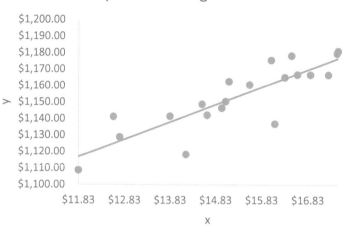

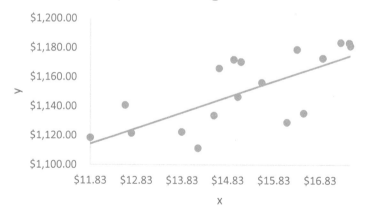

10. Multiple Linear Regression

In our simple linear regression chapter, we explored the relationship between two variables. This chapter had an emphasis on relationships – whether or not the two variables had a statistically significant relationship. We continue our discussion in this chapter, but here, we emphasize predictive ability – finding a model that gives us the highest possible predictive ability. We do this by adding independent variables, which we also refer to as **predictor variables**. The practice of studying such relationships when multiple predictor variables are involved is called **multiple linear regression** or "MLR" for short.

10.1 Improving Predictive Ability

Let us recall our Diet Dr. Pepper example from the simple linear regression chapter. We established a relationship between price and demand for Diet Dr. Pepper. We discovered that the slope term was significant ($t = -3.90$, $p = 0.0045$). We also learned that our R^2 term was 0.6553 – 65.53% of the variation in Demand is explained by Price. This means that 34.47% (1 - 0.6553) of the variation in Demand is explained by something other than Price. If we are interested in estimating or predicting Demand, it seems that we'd like more predictive ability.

10.1.1 Adding More Variables

More predictive ability can be obtained if we add more predictor (independent) variables to our model. This can be done quite easily in Excel – when we are asked for the "X" variables, we simply "paint" all of the independent variables.[6]

Let us continue our Diet Dr. Pepper example from the Simple Linear Regression chapter. This time, however, we will add a predictor variable "Advertising," which represents the number of signs advertising the Diet Dr.

---

[6] To "paint" the necessary predictor variables, they must be in adjacent columns. Otherwise, Excel cannot process them. Columns of predictor variables in non-adjacent columns will not work in Excel.

Pepper. The advertising is done in the proximity of the store. The new data set, then, is as follows:

Price	3.38	3.42	3.48	3.52	3.55	3.55	3.61	3.61	3.67	3.72
Adv.	28	30	28	26	26	28	26	26	26	27
Dem.	83	86	83	81	81	83	81	81	80	80

Table 10.1. Price and Advertising vs. Demand Data for Diet Dr. Pepper

We then ask Excel to perform the linear regression. This time, however, we make certain that both Price and Advertising are treated as "x" variables.

10.1.2 F-Statistic and Regression Output

Prior to discussing the regression output of the example problem, it is appropriate for us to address the hypothesis testing associated with multiple linear regression. When examining the output, the first thing one should consider is the general set of hypotheses that accompany such analyses. The null and alternative hypotheses are as follows:

H_0: The independent variables are related to the
dependent variable   (Eq. 10-1)
H_A: The independent variables are not related
to the dependent variable

The hypotheses stated above are always the case. As such, there is no need to explicitly define them.

To determine whether or not to reject the H_0, we examine the following statistic, which we refer to as the "F-statistic."

$$F = \frac{Explained\ Variation}{Unexplained\ Variation}$$ (Eq. 10-2)

This statistic should not look entirely unfamiliar. We saw something very similar when we discussed the Analysis of Variance. If this ratio is high (the associated p-value being less than some threshold value, such as 0.05), we reject the H_0 and claim that there is a meaningful relationship between the independent and dependent variables.[7]

---

[7] In truth, the significance of the F-statistic in multiple linear regression almost always shows significance, because we are trying to optimize the predictive ability, which strongly implies a significant relationship between the "x" and "y" variables already exists.

For our example problem, our F-statistic is 46.19, with an associated p-value of < 0.0001. Therefore, both Price and Advertising have a meaningful relationship with Demand.

The next order of business is to determine whether or not our predictor variables are statistically significant. Selected regression output is shown in Table 10.2.

	Coefficients	Standard Error	t Stat	P-value
Intercept	79.27	11.87	6.68	0.0003
Price	-6.36	2.30	-2.77	0.0278
Advertisement	0.93	0.18	5.22	0.0012

Table 10.2. Intercept and Slopes for MLR Diet Dr. Pepper Problem

Here we see that the intercept and both slope terms are statistically significant – all p-values are very small. You will also notice that the values of the intercept and the Price slope have changed from the simple linear regression ("SLR") problem. This should not be a surprise, because with the addition of the new term (Advertisement) all other terms will have new values in the pursuit of minimizing the sum of squared errors term.

Now that we can take comfort in that we have a meaningful relationship between Demand and the predictor variables of Price and Advertisements, we can turn our attention to prediction. Excel tells us that our R^2 value is 0.9296. This means that 92.96% of the variation in Demand is explained by both Price and Advertisements. This is a great improvement over the R^2 value from our earlier model, where Price was the only predictor variable for Demand. In general, adding predictor variables to a linear regression will result in an increase in R^2. As such, adding variables to a model improves our predictive ability.

We can now predict Demand by using the predictors of Price and Advertisements via the following equation:

$$\text{Demand} = 79.27 - (6.36)(\text{Price}) + \qquad \text{(Eq. 10-3)}$$
$$(0.93)(\text{Advertisements})$$

We must, however, bear in mind that when predicting; make sure we use values of the predictor variables that are in range of the values from our data set. Otherwise, we are extrapolating, which can provide unreliable results.

10.2 Multicollinearity

Let us consider another example, where I am interested in estimating GMAT Score using the predictor variables of undergraduate GPA and Hours Studying for the GMAT exam. This sounds like a reasonable experiment. It seems reasonable to expect that as both undergraduate GPA and Hours Studying increase, so would the associated GMAT score.

To further investigate this, the data set "GMATExample" has been provided. When performing a multiple linear regression where GMAT score is the dependent (response variable), and GPA and Hours Studying are the predictor variables, we have an F-statistic of 824.93, with an associated p-value < 0.0001. We also have an R^2 value of 0.6238. So far, so good.

When we look at the statistical significance of the individual predictor variables, however, we have the following

	Coefficients	Standard Error	t Stat	P-value
Intercept	-255.47	41.80	-6.11	< 0.0001
GPA	205.93	44.25	4.65	< 0.0001
Hours Studying	2.96	2.35	1.26	0.2091

Table 10.3. Predictor Variables for GMAT Example

When looking at the table above, a problem becomes evident. The slope term for Hours Studying doesn't show statistical significance. We are being told that there is no relationship between Hours Studying and GMAT score. This doesn't make sense. Upon further investigation, a simple linear regression is performed between GMAT score and Hours studying – GPA is excluded from this analysis. This regression reveals that Hours Studying is in fact related to GMAT score (t = 39.94, p < 0.0001).

In summary, multiple linear regression tells us that Hours Studying is not related to GMAT score, while simple linear regression tells us that Hours Studying is related to GMAT score. These conflicting results are a consequence of **multicollinearity** – a strong correlation between predictor variables. While multicollinearity does not have any impact of our ability for prediction, it greatly impedes our ability to interpret individual predictor variables.

10.2.1 Correlation

When we define multicollinearity above, we state that it is the presence of a strong correlation of predictor variables. Now **correlation** must be defined. Correlation is a degree of relationship between variables. That definition sounds eerily familiar – simple linear regression explores relationships between variables. The difference between correlation and simple linear regression is that simple linear regression explains the relationship between slope and intercept, along with the results of associated hypothesis tests, while correlation provides a single standardized statistic describing the relationship between the two variables of interest.

This single standardized statistic used to measure correlation is called the correlation coefficient, ρ. This value of ρ is always in the interval $(-1 \leq \rho \leq 1)$. This value of ρ, intended to measure the correlation between "x" and "y," is determined as follows:

$$\rho = \frac{\sum_{i=1}^{n}(x_i - \bar{x})(y_i - \bar{y})}{\sqrt{\sum_{i=1}^{n}(x_i - \bar{x})^2/(n-1)}\sqrt{\sum_{i=1}^{n}(y_i - \bar{y})^2/(n-1)}} \qquad \text{(Eq. 10-4)}$$

Fortunately, this value is calculated for us using the "=correl(*range1*, *range2*)" function in Excel. Of greater value, however, is the use of the correlation matrix tool available in the Data Analysis Tools. The correlation matrix tool will provide an entire matrix of pairwise correlations between all variables selected. Using this tool for the data in our problem, we have the following:

	GMAT Score	GPA	Hours Studying
GMAT Score	1		
GPA	0.7894	1	
Hours Studying	0.7846	0.9894	1

Table 10.4. Correlation Matrix for GMAT Score Example Problem

10.2.2 Remediation

If we take a close look at our correlation matrix above, we see that we have also included the response variable of GMAT Score. This will be discussed further momentarily. For now, you should take notice of the correlation of 0.9894 – the standardized relationship between the two predictor variables, GPA and hours studying. This means that Hours Studying and GPA are essentially telling us the same thing. Because of this, we have multicollinearity, and when two predictors are highly correlated, our regression output can be counterintuitive. Such is the case here – our multiple regression output tells us that Hours Studying *is not* meaningful, when simple regression tells us Hours Studying *is* meaningful.

What do we do when we get conflicting results like this? There are many opinions on this matter, but I strongly prefer the most **parsimonious** approach. I prefer to remove one of the correlated variables, and let it be explained by the remaining variable. In this situation, it makes the most sense to remove Hours Studying and let it be explained by GPA, because its correlation with GMAT score (the response variable) is less than GPA's correlation with GMAT score (0.7846 < 0.7894).

Because we have removed Hours Studying and let it be explained by GPA, our model reduces to GMAT score as the dependent variable, and with only GPA as our independent variable.

10.3   Parsimony

With having only one predictor variable now, we once again perform a linear regression without Hours Studying as a predictor variable. The results are as follows:

	Coefficients	Std. Error	t Stat	P-value
Intercept	-302.03	19.36	-15.60	< 0.0001
GPA	260.96	6.43	40.59	< 0.0001

Table 10.5. GMAT Score as a Function of GPA Only

Of course, the lone slope of GPA is highly significant (t = 40.59, p < 0.0001). Most importantly, however, is the R^2 value, which is 0.6232 – 62.32% of the variation in GMAT score is explained by GPA. Comparing that to the multiple regression model, where GMAT score is explained by GPA and Hours studying, we have an R^2 of 0.6238. In other words, by removing Hours Studying from our model, we only lose 0.0006 from our R^2 term. A meaningless loss.

This simple example best illustrates the most important aspect of multiple regression, which is **parsimony**. The word "parsimony" is not used much anymore, but it generally implies thrift.[8] In the context of model-fitting, parsimony is intended to suggest the use of as few variables as possible to get the most predictive model. In our present situation, the model with one predictor variable is far superior to the one with two predictor variables because we get the same predictive power with one less term to "worry" about and/or discuss.

10.4 Conclusions

Simple Linear Regression is a tool to explore whether or not relationships exist between variables. With only a single predictor variable, we would be naïve to assume Simple Linear Regression as a good predictive tool. This is where Multiple Linear Regression comes in. Multiple Linear Regression builds on relationships (uncovered by Simple Linear Regression) and attempts to optimize the predictive fit by adding variables. Those variables, however, should be chosen wisely. When the appropriate variables are added, our R^2 term approaches a value of 1.00, resulting in a good predictive model.

If we choose too many predictor variables, we can still have a good predictive model, but we lose our ability to explain our model in a concise manner. We should always attempt to maximize the R^2 term with as few predictor variables as possible.

10.5 Exercises

1. A company that delivers equipment is attempting to understand what determines annual maintenance cost for their fleet of their nine trucks. A data set named "TruckMaintainence" is to be used, where data is given for each truck including the annual maintenance cost for each truck, the number of miles on the truck, and the age of the truck in years. Using $\alpha = 0.05$, please address the following:

---

[8] Charles Dickens often used the word "parsimony" in his work. In the Dickensian context, it implies "thrift" – not spending more money than needed. In our work here, it is important not to use more words and/or variables than needed.

    a. Yes or No: is there an overall relationship between the annual maintenance cost of the truck with the predictor variables of mileage of the truck and the age of the truck.

    b. Justify your response above.

    c. Is the current parsimonious? Why or why not?

    d. What is the most parsimonious model? Justify your response.

2. The data set named "CollegeProbability" contains three variables of data. These variables are "College Prob," "Class Size," and "SAT Score." Definitions of these variables are as follows:

    College Prob: this is the probability that the student in question will attend college.

    Class Size: this is the number of students from the class in which the student in question comes.

    SAT Score: this is the SAT score that the student in question earned.

    For example, the very first data point tells us that the student in question has a 63.52% chance of attending college. This particular student came from a class size of 21, and earned a score of 1232 on the SAT test.

    Your job for this problem is to find the most parsimonious model that explains the probability of attending college. When finding this model, explain the steps you have taken **without** use of Excel terminology.

3. We are interested in determining the driving forces behind mutual fund performance. The attached data set, called "MutualFundPerformance" contains annual return data (in %) for several mutual funds. For each fund, experience (in years) of the mutual fund's manager is provided, along with the fund manager's salary (in $1,000s). The fund type is also provided, which is either a stock fund or bond fund. Using this data, please address the following questions:

    a. Do the experience of the fund manager, the salary of the fund manager, and the fund type have an aggregate relationship with the mutual fund's performance?

    b. Explain the model you used in part "a" above.

    c. Using the model constructed in part "a" above, estimate the fund's return for a bond fund with a fund manager earning a salary of $200,000/year and 12 years experience?

  d. Is multicollinearity a problem? Why or why not?

  e. What is the most parsimonious model that should be used to explain the mutual fund's annual return? Justify your response.

4. I have a data set ("MyStockData") which details daily stock prices of MyStock – a stock that I own. I am trying to use three other stocks to analyze and predict the price of MyStock. Using the attached information, along with a value of $\alpha = 0.01$, please address the following questions:

  a. Yes or No: do Stocks A, B and C have an aggregate relationship with MyStock?

  b. Support your above response.

  c. Yes or No: Is multicollinearity a problem?

  d. Support your above response.

  e. What is the most parsimonious model? Explain your reasoning.

  f. If Stocks A, B and C are priced at $35, $17, $86 respectively, what would expect the price of MyStock to be, when using the most parsimonious model?

5. A beer distributor needs to understand the relationship between the response variable of delivery time and the two predictor variables of distance to travel and the number of cases to deliver. This data is provided ("BeerDistributionTime"). Using this data, please answer the following questions:

  a. Is there an aggregate relationship between delivery time and the two predictor variables of distance to travel and cases to deliver?

  b. Justify your above answer.

  c. Is multicollinearity a problem? Why or why not?

  d. What is the most parsimonious model? Explain your reasoning.

6. A junior golf tournament was held in Walnut Creek, California. There were 500 participants – all of them boys. These participants ranged in age from as young as 13 to as old as 18. For each participant, their 18-hole score was recorded, along with their handicap (a basic measure of the golfer's skill), age, and the number of hours per week

that the golfer of interest practices.   This data is included ("JuniorGolfTournament"). Using this information, please address the following:

    a.   Do age, handicap and hours/week of practice time have an aggregate relationship with the tournament score? Why or why not?

    b. Which predictor variable has the strongest relationship with score? Explain your rationale.

    c.   Is multicollinearity present? Why or why not.

    d. Using the most parsimonious model, estimate the score of a 14-year-old with a handicap of 15 who practices 19 hours/week.

11. Logistic Regression

In this chapter, we conclude our discussion of linear models. Unlike simple linear regression where we essentially study relationships between variables, and unlike multiple linear regression where we are interested with both relationships among variables *and* with prediction, logistic regression is **mainly** concerned with prediction.   Another unique feature of logistic regression is that our dependent variable (response variable) takes on only one of two possible values. Furthermore, this variable is essentially non-numeric in nature; as it takes on values such as pass/fail; true/false; loan/do not loan; promotion/no promotion; cancer/no cancer, etc. We call these types of variables "**binary**" – as only one of two possible outcomes can occur. In practice, these binary variables are coded "1" for "true," and "0" for "false." This is done so that these response variables can be related to a numerical set of predictor variables.

11.1   Predictive Analytics

The term "**predictive analytics**" is, in my opinion, largely due to trends in higher education. The tools used in predictive analytics have been around for a very long time, but in recent years, these tools have been bundled and fashionably referred to as "predictive analytics."

With that said, however, logistic regression falls clearly into the world of predictive analytics. With logistic regression, we can take a list of predictor variables, put them into a model, and predict whether or not something will happen. In the language of regression, these predictor variables are treated as independent variables, whereas the entity being predicted is treated as the dependent variable.

The tool is very useful in commerce. Consider a large bank making a decision on whether or not to approve a loan. When making this decision, there are two possible mistakes that can be made: (1) incorrectly rejecting a loan application and thereby losing profitable interest payments; or (2) incorrectly approving a loan application only to see the borrower default on the loan, thereby losing the amount loaned to the borrower. Because of these two possibilities, the bank obviously wants to make the right decision.

In order to make the right decision, the bank could compile data on past loan applications that were approved. Specific information in this data could include the following: whether or not the borrower defaulted on the loan; the borrower's annual income; the borrower's credit score; the borrower's loan repayment history; and the amount of debt burdening the borrower. These variables could be used to construct a model where the loan default status is the "Y" variable, and the income, credit score, loan history and debt could be used as the "X' variables.

11.2   The Logistic Regression Model

In order to build a predictive model, first we need to understand the basics of the logistic regression model. We start with a linear function that presents the predictor variables (X). Here, we use the value "t" to represent the linear combination of predictor variables:

$$t = \beta_0 + \beta_1 x_1 + \beta_2 x_2 + \; + \beta_m x_m \qquad (11\text{-}1)$$

The value of the intercept and slope terms are typically estimated not by "ordinary least squares," but by an approach called "maximum likelihood estimation," which has an intent similar to ordinary least squares, but uses a different, numerically-based estimation process.

These estimates are used in the following function to compute the probability of the combination of predictor variables to be true at a specific value. This function is as follows:

$$F(x) = \frac{1}{1+e^{-t}} \qquad (11\text{-}2)$$

The above function has the property to lie between 0 and 1. That is:

$$0 \le F(x) \le 1 \qquad (11\text{-}3)$$

This means that the probability of some data point falling into the true category will always be no less than 0, and no more than 1. The cutoff point of being true or false (the "threshold") is determined by the user. A threshold of 0.50 is typically a reasonable value, but this value can be altered depending on the user's intent.

A popular term in logistic regression is called the "logit" function, which is also referred to the "log-odds," and is expressed as follows:

$$\ln\left(\frac{F(x)}{1 - F(x)}\right) = t \tag{11-4}$$

Here, both "t" and the natural log function provide the value for the log-odds. This relationship can be used as an argument in the exponential function, resulting in the following, which presents the "odds."

$$\frac{F(x)}{1 - F(x)} = e^t \tag{11-5}$$

Now that we have a grounding in the mathematics of the logistic regression model, we can apply it to some practical situations.

11.3   The R Statistics Language and Logistic Regression

The above section is for transparency purposes only. That alone is not satisfactory for MBA students to learn about logistic regression. Our world is one of application and interpretation. Because of this, a comprehensive example is needed.

Unfortunately, Excel does not have the capability to perform logistic regression via an ordinary function. Instead, we choose to use the "R" statistical language. The "R" statistical language is a very powerful statistical software package that is freely downloadable. A brief tutorial of R is shown in Appendix B.

11.3.1 Using R for Logistic Regression

To use R for logistic regression, we first take a data set and divide it into two sections. The first section, comprising about 70% of the entire data set, we refer to as the "training" data set. The remaining 30% we refer to as the "testing" data set. We separate the two data sets so that we can build a model on the training data, and then use that model to make predictions using the testing data. This process is often used for diverse predictive analytical processes, including regression-based prediction. Of course, we used this process as well in our coverage of regression – where we first created a model, and then used the model to make predictions using "new" data points.

Figure 13.1 shows the R-code needed to build and analyze a general Logistic Regression model. In this example, italicized terms imply that the creator chooses the model name. Non-italicized terms are required by R. Line 1[9] reads in the training data set, and it is assumed this data set has been saved in "csv" format. Line 2 does the same for the testing data set. Line 3 builds the logistic regression model using the training data set, and saves the result to a variable named *LogModel*. Here, the appropriate response and predictor variables need to be detailed, and we need to state that our response variable is of the binary or "binomial" variety. Line 4 uses the model built in Line 3 and makes predictions based on the test data set. We must specify that we wish to make predictions for the "response" variable. Line 5 requests the "confusion matrix."

---

[9] The R statistical language permits the use of a "comment" sign (" # ") to separate R commands with general comments. This helps with documenting the code to ensure better understanding.

```
>TrainData=read.csv("TrainData.csv")                        # Line 1
>TestData=read.csv("TestData.csv")                          # Line 2
>LogModel=glm(Y ~ X1 + X2 + …, data=TrainData,family="binomial")  # Line 3
>PredModel = predict(LogModel,newdata=TestData,type="response")   # Line 4
>table(TestData$Y, PredModel >= Value)                      # Line 5
```

Figure 11.1 General R Code For Logistic Regression Model

A confusion matrix details the performance of the predictive model. It summarizes all predictions and compares them to their actual classification. A confusion matrix takes on the following form:

Actual Outcome\Predicted Outcome	FALSE	TRUE
0	a_{11}	a_{12}
1	a_{21}	a_{22}

Table 11.1. Confusion Matrix for Logistic Regression

The confusion matrix summarizes the combinations of actual outcomes to predicted outcomes. The "performance" of a confusion matrix can be measured via the following relationship:

$$(a_{11} + a_{22})/(a_{11} + a_{12} + a_{21} + a_{22}) \hspace{2cm} (11\text{-}6)$$

This is the ratio of correct predictions to all predictions. The higher the value, the better the predictive model works.

11.3.2 Specific Logistic Regression Example

For our example, we are given two predictor variables: number of Items to be delivered (Items); and the distance from the delivery point (Distance). Our response variable is "Late," where a value of "1" means a late delivery, and a value of "0" means an on-time delivery. Our R code specific to this model is as follows:

```
>TrainData=read.csv("DeliveryTimesTrain.csv")
>TestData=read.csv("DeliveryTimesTest.csv")
>LogModel=glm(Late ~ Items + Distance, data=TrainData,family="binomial")
>PredModel = predict(LogModel,newdata=TestData,type="response")
>table(TestData$Late,PredModel >= 0.5)
```

Figure 11.2. R Code for Delivery Logistic Regression Model

For details of the logistic regression model we can type "`summary(LogModel)`" in R, and receive the following output:

```
Coefficients:
             Estimate Std. Error z value Pr(>|z|)
(Intercept) -6.925796   1.232591  -5.619 1.92e-08 ***
Items        0.342974   0.086599   3.961 7.48e-05 ***
Distance     0.010419   0.002312   4.507 6.59e-06 ***
---
Signif. codes:  0 '***' 0.001 '**' 0.01 '*' 0.05 '.' 0.1 ' ' 1

(Dispersion parameter for binomial family taken to be 1)

    Null deviance: 182.198  on 132  degrees of freedom
Residual deviance:  61.426  on 130  degrees of freedom
AIC: 67.426

Number of Fisher Scoring iterations: 7
```

Figure 11.3. R Output for Delivery Logistic Regression Model

From this output, we notice that both predictor variables, "Items" and "Late" are statistically significant, as both have p-values < 0.0001. This means that both of them are appropriate predictors for whether or not a delivery is late. The remaining statistics pertain to the overall model fit, via the maximum likelihood estimation approach mentioned earlier. These statistics are beyond the scope of this book.

The fifth and final line of R code asks for a "confusion matrix," a classification summary of actual outcomes and predicted outcomes, in terms of the response variable. This confusion matrix is shown in Table 11.2.

Actual Outcome\Predicted Outcome	FALSE	TRUE
0	19	1
1	2	19

Table 11.2. Confusion Matrix for Delivery Logistic Regression Model

The prediction performance of this model is as follows:

(19 + 19)/(19 + 1 + 2 + 19) = 92.68%

In other words, our logistic regression model correctly predicted 92.68% of the data points from our test data set.

It should be noted that for this problem, a threshold value of 0.5 was used – any predicted value via Equation 11-2 that is equal to or above 0.5 will be predicted a "1," while any predicted value below 0.5 via Equation 11-2 will be classified as "0." The rationale for this is that 0.5 is halfway between 0 and 1. Other threshold values can be used, and it makes good sense to experiment with threshold values that provide the best predictive result.

11.4   Conclusions

Statistics, unlike marketing or IT, is a slowly evolving field in the business school curriculum. This particular chapter, however, is a "newer" part of the discipline, which has become part of the newer field of "business analytics," or "predictive analytics." In truth, logistic regression has been around since 1958. It has been rarely used until recently, however, due to limited hardware and software resources. Thanks to the recent availability of more understandable resources, logistic regression has gained coverage in the business school curriculum.

I see this as a good thing. With this resource in place, we are now able to predict relevant phenomena. This enables banks to make better decisions regarding whether or not to approve loan applications. It better enables companies to market their products to a more specific demographic. It permits medical professionals to predict whether or not an infection or affliction will likely occur. It helps airlines predict overbooking of flights. Consequently, the applications of logistic regression are essentially endless.

11.5   Exercises

1. Use the "LawnMowerTrain.csv" data set and the R statistics language to build a logistic regression model with Income and YardSize as predictor variables and OwnRider as the response variable. Here, each data point represents a homeowner in a certain city. Income is

the annual income, and YardSize is the size of the yard in m^2. An OwnRider value of "1" indicates the homeowner owns a riding mower, while a value of "0" means they do not own a riding mower. Use the constructed logistic regression model and the "LawnMowerTest.csv" data set to predict whether or not the individual owns a riding mower. Which threshold value results in the best predictive ability?

2. Use the "MBAAdmissionsTrain.csv" data set and the R statistics language to build a logistic regression model with GPA and GMAT as predictor variables and Admitted as the response variable. Here, GPA is the undergraduate grade point average of the applicant, while GMAT is the GMAT score of the applicant. Admitted is "1" if the applicant is accepted to the program, while "0" means the applicant is denied admission to the program. Use the "MBAAdmissionTest.csv" to predict admission to the MBA program using the logistic regression model from the training data. What threshold value results in the best predictive ability?

3. A data set was compiled via the IMDB (Internet Movie Data Base). The data set contains the following variables:
   - ID – the movie's ID number
   - Good - "1" if the movies was deemed good; "0" otherwise
   - Length – the length of the film in minutes
   - Budget – the film's budget in US$
   - Votes – the number of votes to cast to determine whether-or-not the movies was deemed "Good."
   - Action – "1" if the movie was in the action genre; 0 otherwise
   - Animation – "1" if the movie was in the animation genre; 0 otherwise
   - Comedy – "1" if the movie was in the comedy genre; 0 otherwise
   - Drama – "1" if the movie was in the drama genre; 0 otherwise
   - Documentary – "1" if the movie was in the documentary genre; 0 otherwise
   - Romance – "1" if the movie was in the romance genre; 0 otherwise

- Short – "1" if the movie was in the short genre; 0 otherwise

Using the "Good" variable as the response variable, and all of the other variables (except for ID) as predictor variables, build a logistic regression model using the "MovieTrain.csv" data set. Then use the logistic regression model and the "MovieTest.csv" data set to predict whether or not a movie is classified as Good. What threshold results in the best predictive ability?

4. A data set has been compiled that explores the factors associated with low birth weight in the United States. The relevant variables are as follows:
   - ID – the observation's ID number
   - LowBirthWt – "1" if the baby's birth weight is low; 0 otherwise
   - MotherAge – age of the mother giving birth
   - MotherWeight – the weight of the mother giving birth
   - Race – the race of the mother ("1" for Caucasian; "2" for African-American; "3" for other)
   - Smoker – "1" if the mother is a smoker; 0 otherwise
   - PrematureLabor – "1" if the baby was born prematurely; 0 otherwise
   - Hypertension – "1" if the mother suffers from hypertension; 0 otherwise
   - UterineIrratibility – "1" if the mother suffers from uterine irritability; 0 otherwise
   - PhysicianVisits – the number of mother visits to the physician during pregnancy

Using the "LowBirthWt" variable as the response variable, and all of the other variables (except for ID) as predictor variables, build a logistic regression model using the "BirthWeightTrain.csv" data set. Then use the logistic regression model and the "BirthWeightTest.csv" data set to predict whether or not a baby has a low birth weight. What threshold results in the best predictive ability?

12.   Business Forecasting

We now address a topic that technically does not fit into the world of traditional "statistics," but is part of Quantitative Methods – the very large topic of business forecasting. Business forecasting is where we take historical data and "extrapolate" it into the future. With the prediction we did in Simple and Multiple Linear Regression, we "interpolated." That is, we took data, built a model, and estimated *within* the boundaries of the data we have. With forecasting, we take data, build a model, and estimate *beyond* the boundaries of the data we have. That is, we estimate what will happen in the future based upon historical data we have gathered an analyzed.

There are many forecasting tools, but we will concentrate on the regression-based tools, given that we now have a basic understanding of how regression works.

12.1   Time Series Analysis

We can think of forecasting as "time series analysis." A **time series** is a collection of historical data. This historical data collection has an observation for some regular time interval, such as daily, weekly, monthly, etc. These time intervals must be evenly spaced for our presented methodology to work properly.

12.2   Simple Forecasting Tools

Prior to our delving into the regression-based forecasting tools, we will briefly cover the simple forecasting tools – the moving average tools, where we simply extrapolate into the future by averaging historical data. We will start by considering the simple times series shown here:

Day	1	2	3	4	5	6	7	8
Demand	12	12	13	15	16	16	19	20

Table 12.1. Time Series Data for Forecasting Problem

For these problems, we will introduce the terms D_t and F_t, which mean demand for period t and the Forecast for period t.

12.2.1 Simple Moving Average

The **simple moving average** forecasting approach is the simplest approach imaginable. We simply select the most recent past values of demand and average them. The number of periods we select to average is determined by the forecaster. For example, we could choose three **averaging periods**, and the resultant forecast for the next period, F_9, will be as follows:

$$F_9 = (D_8 + D_7 + D_6)/3 = (20 + 19 + 16) / 3 = 18.33 \qquad \text{(Eq. 12-1)}$$

12.2.2 Weighted Moving Average

One of the unpleasant realities of the Simple Moving Average Approach is that each historical period is considered just as important as the others. This may not be appropriate, as the most recent values should probably have the most to say about the forecast. This is where the weighted moving average approach may be an improvement. Why not "weight" historical periods according to relative importance. For our example problem, still using three averaging periods, I will "weight" the most recent period 0.5, the period prior to that 0.3 and the period prior to that 0.2. Notice how these weight sums to one. Our forecast then becomes:

$$F_9 = .5D_8 + .3D_7 + .3D_6 = .5(20) + .3(19) + .3(16) = 17.7 \qquad \text{(Eq. 12-2)}$$

This forecast may be better thought out than the simple moving average, due to its ability to treat historical periods as-needed.

12.2.3 Differencing

Unfortunately, neither of the forecasting approaches above is reliable. The reason is that whatever value we forecast into the future, that value will always be somewhere between the minimum and maximum values that we use for our average. In short, we are interpolating, when there are times we need to be extrapolating.

The concept of **differencing** enables us to extrapolate. If we take the difference in demand (or whatever entity we are trying to forecast) from one period and the prior period, and average all of those periodic differences, we have the average change per time unit. If we let Δ_t represent the difference for period t, we have the following:

$$\Delta_t = D_t - D_{t-1} \qquad \text{(Eq. 12-3)}$$

$$\bar{\Delta}= \frac{1}{n-1}\sum_{t=2}^{n} \Delta_t \qquad\qquad \text{(Eq. 12-4)}$$

For this notation, n represents the number of periods. For our example, period differences are shown in the table below:

Day	1	2	3	4	5	6	7	8
Demand	12	12	13	15	16	16	19	20
Difference		0	1	2	1	0	3	1

Table 12.2. Time Series Data for Forecasting Problem

When we average these differences, we have an average difference of 1.42. This means that we can expect demand to increase 1.42 units each period. Using this logic, our forecast for period 9 can be $F_9 = D_8 + \bar{\Delta} = 20 + 1.42 = 21.42$.

Another advantage differencing has over the moving average approaches is that differencing permits us to forecast multiple periods into the future, while the moving average approaches only permit us to forecast a single period into the future.

12.3   Regression Based Forecasting

Differencing is far better than the moving average approaches, but it nevertheless is naive in that fails to minimize the sum of squared errors, provided by regression. Regression based forecasting can take care of this for us when we exploit the model where demand is a function of the time period. In other words, we treat our time period as the independent variable and we treat our Demand value as the dependent variable. Once we have estimates of slope and intercept, we can "fit" values of demand:

$$\hat{D}_t = \text{Intercept} + \text{Slope}\,(t) \qquad\qquad \text{(Eq. 12-5)}$$

Comparing our values of actual demand, D_t, with those "fitted," we can calculate the error for each time period, which in forecasting, we call this the absolute deviation (AD_t):

$$AD_t = \left| D_t - \hat{D}_t \right| \qquad\qquad \text{(Eq. 12-6)}$$

The mean absolute deviation (*MAD*) is simply the average of the AD values for all time periods:

$$MAD = \frac{1}{n}\sum_{t=1}^{n} AD_t \qquad \text{(Eq. 12-7)}$$

Knowing the forecast error (MAD), we can use our "fit" model above to forecast into the future:

$$F_t = \text{Intercept} + \text{Slope}\,(t) \qquad \text{(Eq. 12-8)}$$

12.3.1 Linear Trends

Continuing with the example we used for the other forecasting approaches, simple linear regression forecasting for the data set provides an intercept of 9.96 and a slope of 1.20, or more formally, we can use the following for forecasting into the next period:

$$F_t = 9.96 + 1.20t \qquad \text{(Eq. 12-9)}$$

The actual "fits" and absolute deviation values are below.

Day	1	2	3	4	5	6	7	8
D_t	12	12	13	15	16	16	19	20
$\widehat{D}_t$	11.17	12.37	13.57	14.77	15.98	17.18	18.38	19.58
AD_t	0.83	0.37	0.57	0.23	0.02	1.18	0.62	0.42

Table 12.3. Regression Forecasting Results for Example Problem

Figure 11.1 shows a time series plot of the given data along with the regression forecasting line, where we have forecast two periods into the future ($F_9 = 20.79$, $F_{10} = 21.99$).

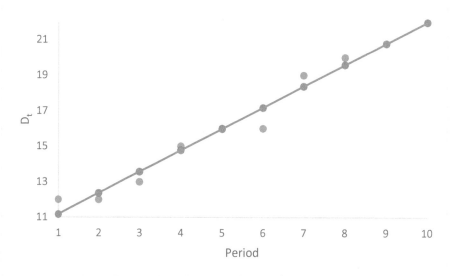

Figure 12.1. Simple Linear Regression Forecasting

One might note how the forecast line is simply a continuation of the trend, which we quantified via simple linear regression.

12.3.2 Nonlinear Trends

Sometimes our trend is not linear. Consider the data shown in the scatter plot, and the fitted regression line in Figure 12.2.

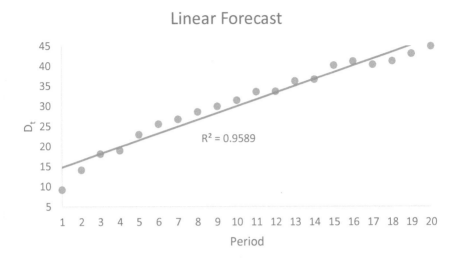

Figure 12.2. Nonlinear Data with Linear Fit

Upon careful inspection, you might notice that the trend line overestimates the first few periods, underestimates the middle periods, and once again overestimates the latter periods. This suggests that the trend is nonlinear. Perhaps we are "splitting hairs" here, but one can make a very reasonable argument for a nonlinear trend. When this occurs, we can use multiple linear regression as a means to achieve "nonlinear regression." We can do this by creating a new independent variable called t^2, which is simply the period multiplied by itself and used as a predictor variable, resulting in the following general equation:

$$\hat{D}_t = a + b_1 t^2 + b_2 t \qquad \text{(Eq. 12-10)}$$

Using multiple regression to estimate the intercept and slope terms, we have the following model we can use for forecasting:

$$F_t = 8.57 - 0.06t^2 + 2.92t \qquad \text{(Eq. 12-11)}$$

A time series plot of the fitted model is shown in Figure 12.3.

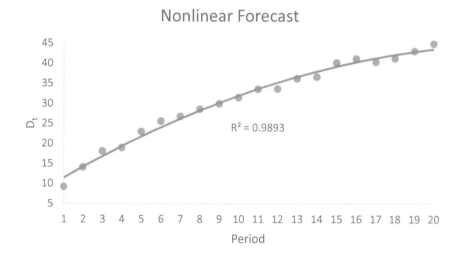

Figure 12.3. Nonlinear Data with Nonlinear Fit

Two things should be noted from inspection of Figure 12.3. First, notice how the nonlinear fit better captures the data points than does the line via the simple regression model. Second, notice how the associated R^2 term has increased about 0.03 from the simple regression model.

12.3.3 Microsoft Excel and Forecasting

One of Microsoft Excel's greatest attributes is that it does an excellent job at finding the best fit for a data set. Given a plot of data, right-clicking the mouse button and selecting "Add Trendline" opens up an almost infinite collection of tools to select the best "fit" for the given data set. One can select from a straight line, a polynomial curve, a power curve, a logarithmic curve, an exponential curve, etc. From these choices, there are a variety of parameters to choose from as well. It is worth experimenting with these tools and options to find the best fit. Be warned, however, the principle of parsimony should always apply – always select a model that can be explained.

Excel's trendline options are many. This is a very powerful tool. Nevertheless, as powerful as this tool is, performing regression via the Analysis Tools as we have done throughout this book is still needed to determine whether or not the model parameters (slope, etc.) are statistically significant.

12.4   Seasonality in Forecasting

The final forecasting topic we cover is seasonal forecasting. Seasonality exists in almost all forms of commerce. For example, champagne sales are higher than average in December. Retail stores are busy in November and December. More barbeque sauce is sold in the summer months compared to other parts of the year. Tax accountants are very busy in March and April. Maine has lots of tourists in the summer months, while Florida has lots of tourists in the winter months. This list could go on and on, but seasonality is a powerful force of nature. It is important we have the ability to forecast in the presence of seasonality.

This can be accomplished via a variety of tools, but we will use **seasonalized time series regression forecasting** here. Conceptually, this is a straightforward process. We will illustrate this with an example via a seasonal time series shown in Table 12.4.

Quarter	Period	Year 1 Demand	Period	Year 2 Demand	Period	Year 3 Demand
1	1	85	5	93	9	96
2	2	118	6	130	10	133
3	3	83	7	89	11	95
4	4	69	8	74	12	75

Table 12.4. Seasonal Time Series Data

This time series is organized slightly differently from what we've seen thus far. Each row indicates the "quarter." Each pair of columns indicates the period number and year. The table shows that there are three years of quarterly data, for twelve total observations. Quarters are organized by row, and year is organized by column.

12.4.1 Order of Seasonality

We first need to determine the "order" of seasonality. The order of seasonality is how many individual periods there are for each cycle. If we have monthly data, the order of seasonality is twelve. If we have hourly data, the order of seasonality is twenty-four. For our example, we have quarterly data, so the order of seasonality is four. The order of seasonality can be determined by either examining a time series plot or by understanding how many time periods there are for each temporal cycle.

Given that we know the order of seasonality for our problem is four, we compute the **seasonal index** for each season – quarters for our example. The seasonal index for a specific season is the average for that specific season divided by the average of all the given data. For example, the seasonal index for January would be for the average for all January observations divided by the average for all data. For quarters, the seasonal index for the first quarter would be the average value of the first quarter data divided by the average of all data. Mathematically, we can pursue this as follows: there are n rows (a row for each quarter, and i is the row index), and there are m columns (a column for each year, and j is the column index). The value of quantity demand for the jth quarter for year i will be represented by D_{ij}. Seasonal indices (SI_j) are as follows:

$$SI_i = \frac{\left(\sum_{j=1}^{m} D_{ij}\right)/m}{\left(\sum_{j=1}^{m} \sum_{i=1}^{n} D_{ij}\right)/mn} \qquad (12\text{-}12)$$

Using this formula, we can calculate the seasonal indices for our example problem, which are shown in Table 12.5.

Quarter	Period	Year 1 Dem.	Period	Year 2 Dem.	Period	Year 3 Dem.	SI
1	1	85	5	93	9	96	0.96
2	2	118	6	130	10	133	1.34
3	3	83	7	89	11	95	0.94
4	4	69	8	74	12	75	0.76

Table 12.5. Seasonal Indices for Time Series Data

12.4.2 De-Seasonalize Data

The seasonal indices display the relative contribution each season makes to the aggregate demand. You will see from our calculations that the second quarter is the "busy" quarter, compared to quarters 1, 3 and 4.

The next step is to "de-seasonalize" the data by taking each observation and dividing it by its appropriate seasonal index. The de-seasonalized data for the ith quarter for the jth year will be represented by DS_{ij}, and is calculated as follows:

$$DS_{ij} = \frac{D_{ij}}{SI_i} \qquad (12\text{-}13)$$

The formula above filters out the seasonality, and isolates any trend which may exist, and linear regression is the sensible tool of choice to capture a trend.

12.4.3 Capture Trend

To capture the trend, we simply fit a model where the de-seasonalized data is the dependent variable and the independent variable is the time period. Before showing this model, however, we need to convert our de-seasonalized data from DS_{ij} form to DS_t form. We do this via the following:

$$t = nj + i, \forall i = 1, \dots n; \ \forall j = 0, \dots, m - 1 \qquad (12\text{-}14)$$

Do not place too much concern with the above formula – the appropriate period numbers (t) are listed next to the actual demand values. We can fit the linear model to capture the trend exposed by our de-seasonalized data:

$$\widehat{DS}_t = a + bt \qquad (12\text{-}15)$$

Fitting this model with our de-seasonalized data, we have captured the trend, with an intercept of 87.12 and a slope of 1.21, resulting in the following fit/forecast model:

$$F_t = 87.12 + 1.21t \qquad (12\text{-}16)$$

Figure 12.4 shows what we've accomplished so far. It is important to note how de-seasonalizing the data results in removal of the cycles and isolates only the trend.

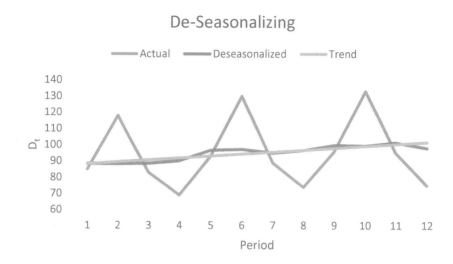

De-Seasonalizing

Figure 12.4. De-Seasonalizing Quarterly Data

12.4.4 Fit and Forecast

The final step to this forecasting approach is to re-incorporate seasonality and then extrapolate our estimates into the future. First, let us perform **back-forecasting** to compare our estimates with the actual data. To do this, we simply multiply our trend by the appropriate seasonal index:

$$F_t = (87.12 + 1.21t)SI_i \qquad (12\text{-}17)$$

Here, SI_i is the appropriate seasonal index corresponding with period t. Simply put, multiplying the fitted trend by the appropriate seasonal index puts the seasonality "back in." We can then determine the MAD by comparing the **back-forecasts** to the given data:

$$MAD = \frac{1}{P}\sum_{t=1}^{P}|D_t - F_t| \qquad (12\text{-}18)$$

For our example, the MAD is 1.55. On average, our back-forecast is 1.55 units different from the actual.

At this point, to forecast, we only need to "extend" our line into the future by adding new values of t, and using the appropriate SI_i values to re-seasonalize our data, along with our trend model. A comparison of our actual data and our fit/forecast data one year into the future is shown below. Notice how closely the fit/forecast line matches up with the actual values.

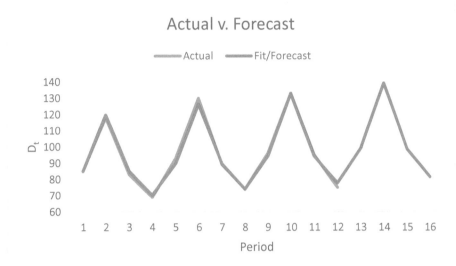

Figure 12.5. Actual Data Compared to Fit/Forecast

The notation in this section has been complicated due to the fact that we must change from double-subscripted notation ("ij") to time-series notation ("t"). Because of this complicating force, the Appendix is provided for a more deliberated pursuit of this example problem.

12.5 Parsimony

There is a very large arsenal of forecasting tools. In this chapter, we have covered some simple, yet very useful tools. There is always a temptation to increase the R^2 or decrease the MAD term a little bit so as to boast a better forecast. When forecasting, let us remember that we may have to explain the details of our forecasting approach to someone else – perhaps someone who is not quantitatively versed. Because of this, it is very important to keep our forecasts as straightforward as possible. Your objective should not be to "impress" the customer, but to "inform" the customer.

Parsimony should always rule the day. Always.

12.6 Conclusions

Forecasting is a very powerful topic. Even though this book is introductory in nature, we have covered linear forecasting, nonlinear forecasting and seasonal forecasting. With just a little bit of practice and experience, these tools can provide immense value to organizations.

My experience in industry taught me that forecasting is one thing that is done quite poorly. With just a bit of practice from the tools presented here, poor forecasting can be greatly improved.

The "real-world" aspect of forecasting needs to be addressed via a personal experience. Several years ago, I was hired by a public utility company in northern Maine to provide revenue forecasts. I used a sophisticated forecasting technique, and excitedly reported my results to the client. The client was happy with the work, but then proceeded to tell me that we needed to "tweak" the forecasts based on things he thought would happen in the future – litigation related to pricing, availability of electricity, etc. Because of these real world issues with which I was unfamiliar, we increased our forecast 5% for one month, and decreased our forecast 3% for another month, etc. In other words, we adjusted the scientific forecasts to accommodate realistic issues. As the years have passed, this particular experience has become very salient to me. The forecasting we have covered in chapter has been a scientific pursuit, but the best forecasts should always consider real world issues that can occur.

12.7 Exercises

1. The time series "SeriesG" documents domestic air travelers (in 1,000s) from January, 1959 to December, 1970. Find the most appropriate forecasting model and forecast domestic air travel for all months of 1971.
2. The time series "SnowShovels" shows demand for snow shovels from January, 2006 through December, 2010. Find the most appropriate

forecasting model, and forecast snow shovel demand for all months of 2011.

3. The time series "TimeSeries1" shows Advertising dollars for a specific day, and the sales the following day. Using the most appropriate forecasting model, explain the relationship between Advertising dollars and the next day's sales.

4. The time series "TimeSeries2" shows" monthly demand for a certain entity. Find the most appropriate forecasting model and forecast demand one year into the future.

5. JimBob's Video Shoppe is interested in forecasting quarterly rentals from the following data set:

Year	Quarter 1	Quarter 2	Quarter 3	Quarter 4
2010	2402	1821	1412	2937
2011	1967	1582	1510	2928
2012	2074	1838	1390	3142
2013	2104	1779	1390	2811

Use the provided data set to forecast one year into the future.

6. A dentist's office bills on a bi-monthly basis. This means every two months. January/February is one billing period, March/April is the next billing period, etc. The "DentistBilling" data set details billing for the most recent three years: 2010, 2011 and 2012. Choose the most appropriate model and forecast one period into the future.

13. Decision Tree Analysis

Life is filled with decision-making. Some decisions are easy, some are difficult. In this chapter, we deal with the difficult decisions – at least from a quantitative standpoint. An example of an easy decision is one where we are offered two jobs – we will call them A and B. If jobs A and B are identical in every aspect, with the exception of compensation, we take the job offering the highest compensation. This decision is trivial.

Let's take this example one step further. Job A offers more compensation than does Job B, but Job B looks more promising in terms of professional growth. What is the likelihood for growth regarding Job B? How much growth is associated with Job B? All of a sudden this decision becomes less trivial because of the uncertainty associated with future professional growth opportunities. In short, we are confronted with a difficult decision.

In this chapter, we explore the tools used to analyze decisions that involved uncertainty.

13.1 Decision Trees

To address these decisions involving uncertainty, we first itemize the list of options and call them **alternatives**. We will assume there are n unique alternatives, and refer to alternative i as a_i. Each alternative has an uncertain **outcome** that does not present itself until after the decision is made. We will assume that there are m possible outcomes for each alternative. Each outcome has a certain probability of occurring. We will refer to the probability of outcome j occurring as p_j. Each outcome has an associated **payoff**. We will refer to the payoff associated with alternative i and outcome j as P_{ij}.

We combine all of this information via a decision tree – a graphical representation of all alternatives and associated outcomes and payoffs. A rectangular node represents where a decision needs to be made. A round node represents an outcome of which we are uncertain. Each outcome has some probability of occurring. After the uncertainty is represented, we are shown the payoff in monetary or similar units.

As an example, consider the decision of whether or not to bring an umbrella to work in the morning. There are two alternatives: bring an umbrella or do not bring an umbrella. For each alternative, there is uncertainty: rain or no rain. Our decision is influenced by the possible outcomes. This problem is represented by the decision tree shown in Figure 10.1

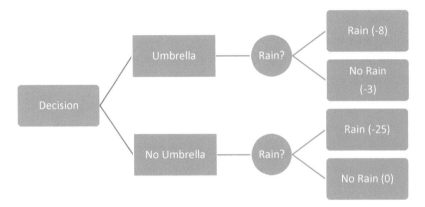

Figure 13.1. Decision Tree for Umbrella Problem

There are four outcomes for this problem: (1) we bring an umbrella and it rains; (2) we bring an umbrella and it does not rain; (3) we do not bring an umbrella and it rains; and (4) we do not bring an umbrella and it rains. The payoffs associated with these outcomes are: -8, -3 -25 and 0. These payoffs are in units of **utility** – a non-monetary unit associated with success. "Utility" is often used economics.

13.2 Decision Strategies

We are not unable to make a decision (choose an alternative) until we know what it is we wish to accomplish. As such, prior to making a decision, we need to pursue a particular strategy. In decision analysis, there are several strategies, but we will cover the three most basic here.

13.2.1 Optimistic Strategy ("Maximax")

If we are optimistic, we assume the best will happen. In this case, we choose our alternative assuming the best possible outcome will occur. This means that for each alternative, we select the most favorable outcome and then select the alternative with the best overall outcome. For our umbrella problem, then, we choose accordingly:

$$Max[max(-8, -3), max(-25, 0)] \qquad \text{(Eq. 13-1)}$$

This simplifies to the following:

$$Max[-3, 0] = 0 \qquad \text{(Eq. 13-2)}$$

This "**maximax**" value of 0 is the payoff associated with not bringing an umbrella, because we assume there will be no rain. The upshot of this is that under the optimistic strategy, we choose not to bring an umbrella because we don't think it is going to rain.

13.2.2 Pessimistic Strategy ("Maximin")

If we are pessimistic, we assume the worst will happen, and the make the best decision accordingly. This means that for each alternative, we assume the worst will happen, and then choose the alternative that provides us with the best result. For our umbrella problem, we proceed as follows:

$$Max[min(-8, -3), min(-25, 0)] \qquad \text{(Eq. 13-3)}$$

This simplifies to the following:

$$Max[-8, -25] = -8 \qquad \text{(Eq. 13-4)}$$

The "**maximin**" value here is -8, the payoff associated with bringing an umbrella when it rains. This means that the best pessimistic decision is to bring an umbrella because we think it will rain.

13.2.3 Expected Value Strategy

The first two strategies covered are important strategies, but for this example, the results are self-obviating – the optimist will not bring an umbrella because they do not think it will rain, while the pessimist will bring an umbrella because they think it will rain.

We will now examine another strategy that is more rooted in mathematics and specifically probability. We will explore the expected value strategy, which is based on what we expect each alternative's value to be. The expected value for alternative a_i is represented as $E(a_i)$ and is determined as follows:

$$E(a_i) = \sum_{j=1}^{m} p_j P_{ij}$$

(Eq. 13-5)

For our umbrella problem, we will assume a probability of rain to be 0.25, which implies a probability of no rain as 0.75.

For the umbrella alternative, our expected value is:

$$(.25)(-8) + (.75)(-3) = -4.25 \qquad \text{(Eq. 13-6)}$$

For the no umbrella alternative, our expected value is:

$$(.25)(-25) + (.75)(0) = -6.25 \qquad \text{(Eq. 13-7)}$$

Comparing the expected values of the two alternatives, we wish to maximize:

$$\text{Max}[-4.25, -6.25] = -4.25 \qquad \text{(Eq. 13-8)}$$

Our best alternative has an expected value of -4.25, and is associated with the "no umbrella alternative." As such, using expected value, we should not bring the umbrella. We will call this value of -4.25 as the **expected value**.

13.3   Expected Value of Perfect Information

We can take our discussion of expected value one step further. When we calculated our expected value (EV) above, we essentially calculated the **expected value under uncertainty** because we were not certain what would happen in the future. Let's assume for a moment that we have the ability to make our decision with advanced knowledge of what will happen. For example, if we knew in advance it was going to rain, we would bring our umbrella, and if we knew in advance it was not going to rain, we would not bring our umbrella. In terms of the mathematical approach to this problem, the **expected value under certainty** would be as follows:

$$EVUC = \sum_{j=1}^{m} p_j \cdot \max_i(P_{ij})$$

(Eq. 13-9)

For our umbrella problem, assume we have advance knowledge that it will rain. With that knowledge, we select an umbrella as that payoff is better than the payoff associated with not bringing un umbrella when it rains (max[-8, -25] = -8). With advance knowledge that it will not rain, we would choose not to bring an umbrella because of the higher payoff (max[-3, 0] = 0). Because our advance knowledge of rain will occur 25% of the time, and advance knowledge of no rain will occur 75% of the time, our expected value under certainty value is as follows:

$$EVUC = (-8)(.25) + (0)(.75) = -2 \qquad \text{(Eq. 13-10)}$$

In other words, under certainty – with advance knowledge of what will happen, we expect a payoff of -2.

To summarize, under uncertainty, we have an expected value of -4.25. We refer to this value as the expected value, or the **expected value under uncertainty** (EVUU). Under certainty, we have an expected value of -2. We call this the expected value under certainty (EVUC). The difference between these two values is referred to as the expected value with perfect information (EVPI). Mathematically, this value is as follows:

$$EVPI = EVUC - EVUU \qquad \text{(Eq. 13-11)}$$

For our example, the EVPI is -2 - (-4.25) = 2.25. This value is always positive, and numerically represents the difference between being certain and being uncertain. Another way to interpret this is maximum amount you should "pay" to eliminate uncertainty.

13.4   An Example

Let is consider a monetary example with three investment alternatives: Bonds, Stocks and CDs. Each alternative has three possible outcomes: growth, stagnation and inflation. We assume that the probability of growth is 50%, the probability of stagnation is 30%, and the probability of inflation is 20%. Figure 10.2 shows the details of this problem, including payoffs in decision tree format.

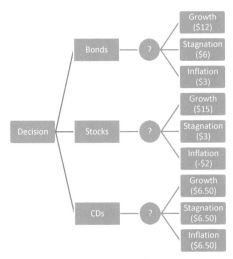

Figure 13.2. Decision Tree for Investment Problem

Table 13.1 displays this data in table format for easy calculations.

Alternative	Outcomes			Results		
	Growth (p = 0.5)	Stag. (p = 0.3)	Inflation (p = 0.2)	Max	Min	EVUU
Bonds	$12	$6	$3	$12	$3	$8.4
Stocks	$15	$3	-$2	$15	-$2	$8
CDs	$6.5	$6.5	$6.5	$15	$6.5	$6.5
Max Val.	$15	$6.5	$6.5	$15	$6.5	$8.4
Decision	N/A			Stocks	CDs	Bonds

Table 13.1. Details of Monetary Example Decision Tree Problem

For each alternative, the maximum, minimum and expected value payoffs have been determined. The optimist would choose Stocks because $15, the best possible outcome would occur via the Stocks decision. The pessimist would choose CDs, because $6.5 is the best outcome assuming the worst will happen. When pursuing expected value, Bonds is the best decision, because they provide the highest expected value ($8.4).

The expected value under certainty is as follows:

$$EVUC = 15(0.5) + 6.5(0.3) + 6.5(0.3) = 10.75 \qquad \text{(Eq. 13-12)}$$

Now that we understand the expected value under uncertainty is $8.4 and the expected value under certainty is $10.75, we can calculate the expected value of perfect information as ($10.75 − $8.4 = $2.35). To put this result into a monetary context, we can say that the value of eliminating uncertainty is $2.35 – if we hired someone with the ability to somehow remove uncertainty from our problem, we should pay them no more than $2.35 for their services.

13.5 Conclusions

Decision analysis is an important topic in that it bridges the theoretical and applied worlds. I have personally never constructed a decision tree for a decision that I have needed to make. Nevertheless, a decision tree does structure a decision in terms of options, associated uncertainties and their interrelationships, which is important.

Another thing worth considering is that our payoffs are subjected to interpretation. In our umbrella example, we talk about how being in the rain without an umbrella is somehow a "bad" thing. That is basically stated from the perspective of someone traveling to work or classes at the university. Imagine, however, a nervous farmer in South Dakota worried about a dried-out corn crop in August. If that farmer is caught in a downpour without an umbrella will they be upset? Of course not – they will be relieved and happy. This point needs to be made because payoffs need to be valued from the proper perspective.

Another issue to consider is the concept of outcomes. In our example problems, our outcomes are "discrete" – either a specific outcome occurs or does not occur. In reality that is not the case. For our example problem, we have outcomes that state it is either raining or it is not raining. Unfortunately, there are times, especially in places like Seattle, San Francisco or London where we are in a fog, and we're not sure if it is raining or not – such situations are not discrete. The thinking behind quantification of payoffs and outcomes is part of a larger social science known as decision/utility theory.

Finally, it is worth mentioning the concept of expected value with perfect information. As we define this concept, we describe it as the value of eliminating uncertainty. In reality, of course, we cannot eliminate uncertainty.

If we had that ability, there is essentially no reason in having this book. Nevertheless, we do perform better as organizations and individuals if we can minimize uncertainty. Consider financial service companies like ETrade and TDAmeritrade. These corporations, along with others, boast of research they provide which "reduces" uncertainty, and subsequently improving portfolio performance. They are essentially claiming that they have the ability to reduce uncertainty. Regardless of whether or not these vague claims are true, they do entice the investor to consider the value of the advertised research – the claim of reduced uncertainty, which lies at the heart of decision analysis.

13.6   Exercises

For these questions, address the following: state what the optimist would do; state what the pessimist would do; state what one would do using expected value as a strategy; and state the expected value of perfect information.

1. I have some money to invest, and I have three investment options: ChemicalBrothers, MötleyCrüe, and ConcreteBlonde. ChemicalBrothers has a payoff of $10 when a good market occurs, and a loss of $5 when a bad market occurs. MötleyCrüe has a payoff of $7 when a good market occurs, and a loss of $4 when a bad market occurs. ConcreteBlonde has a payoff of $5 when a good market occurs, and a loss of $2 when a bad market occurs. A good market has a 40% chance of occurring.

2. You have been given some money to invest, and you are considering three different options for your investment choice: AlphaStuds, BetaStuds and GammaStuds. Under a favorable market, AlphaStuds will return $100, but lose $30 under an unfavorable market. Under a favorable market, BetaStuds will return $75, but lose $25 under an unfavorable market. GammaStuds will return $60 under a favorable market, but lose $15 under an unfavorable market. A favorable market has a 60% of occurring, while an unfavorable market has a 40% chance of occurring. All money must be invested in one of the three options – distributing the investment among multiple investments is not permitted.

3. I have some money to invest. I will invest all of it in either RustStuds or JetElectro. RustStuds will return a gain of $10 in a favorable market and a loss of $3 in an unfavorable market. JetElectro will return a gain $14 in a favorable market, and a loss of $5 in an unfavorable market. The probability of the market being favorable is 60%, while there is a 40% probability of an unfavorable market.

4. I have some money to invest, and I'm considering three possible investments: AcmeCorp, BestCorp, and CoolioCorp. When the return is favorable, I can expect a $1,000 payoff from AcmeCorp, a $500 return from BestCorp, and a $400 return from CoolioCorp. When the return is unfavorable, I can expect a loss of $300 from AcmeCorp, a loss of $200 from BestCorp, and a loss of $100 from CoolioCorp. There is a 55% probability of a favorable return and a 45% probability of an unfavorable return.

5. I have $1M to invest. I have narrowed my investment choices down to two possible alternatives: AlphaTron and OmegaTron. I must invest all of the $1M in one of the securities – mixing the investment between the two securities is not permitted. Under good market conditions, AlphaTron will provide a return of $100K, while OmegaTron will provide a return of $60K. Under average market conditions, AlphaTron will provide a return of $20K, while OmegaTron will provide a return of $10K. Under bad market conditions, AlphaTron will lose $60K, while OmegaTron will lose $30K. Good market conditions are estimated to occur with a 40% probability, average and bad market conditions are each estimated to occur with a 30% probability.

Appendix A. Development of Seasonal Forecasting Problem

Consider the data set shown in the forecasting chapter:

Quarter	t	D_t	t	D_t	t	D_t	Avg.	SI
1	1	85	5	93	9	96	91.33	0.96
2	2	118	6	130	10	133	127.00	1.34
3	3	83	7	89	11	95	89.00	0.94
4	4	69	8	74	12	75	72.67	0.76

Table 1. Given Data with Seasonal Indices Calculated

This table is different in that instead of Demand in double-subscripted notation, it is subscripted by time period, while the table's rows are organized by quarter. This easily lets us calculate seasonal averages and seasonal indices, which are shown. The table is not re-organized so that all time periods are in a single column.

Period	SI	D_t	DS_t
1	0.96	85	88.54
2	1.34	118	88.06
3	0.94	83	88.30
4	0.76	69	90.79
5	0.96	93	96.88
6	1.34	130	97.01
7	0.94	89	94.68
8	0.76	74	97.37
9	0.96	96	100.00
10	1.34	133	99.25
11	0.94	95	101.06
12	0.76	75	98.68

Table 2. De-Seasonalized Data

From the de-seasonlized data, we capture the trend, having an intercept of 87.12 and a slope of 1.21. Applying these terms to the de-seasonalized data, we have the following fitted trend:

Period	SI	D_t	DS_t	Trend
1	0.96	85	88.54	88.33
2	1.34	118	88.06	89.54
3	0.94	83	88.30	90.75
4	0.76	69	90.79	91.96
5	0.96	93	96.88	93.17
6	1.34	130	97.01	94.38
7	0.94	89	94.68	95.59
8	0.76	74	97.37	96.8
9	0.96	96	100.00	98.01
10	1.34	133	99.25	99.22
11	0.94	95	101.06	100.43
12	0.76	75	98.68	101.64

Table 3. Fitted Trend

The final step in this process is to re-incorporate our seasonality, and extend our fitted trend into the future. This is shown below:

Period	SI	D_t	DS_t	Trend	Fit/Forecast
1	0.96	85	88.54	88.33	84.80
2	1.34	118	88.06	89.54	119.98
3	0.94	83	88.30	90.75	85.31
4	0.76	69	90.79	91.96	69.89
5	0.96	93	96.88	93.17	89.44
6	1.34	130	97.01	94.38	126.47
7	0.94	89	94.68	95.59	89.85
8	0.76	74	97.37	96.8	73.57
9	0.96	96	100.00	98.01	94.09
10	1.34	133	99.25	99.22	132.95
11	0.94	95	101.06	100.43	94.40
12	0.76	75	98.68	101.64	77.25
13	0.96			102.85	98.74
14	1.34			104.06	139.44
15	0.94			105.27	98.95
16	0.76			106.48	80.92

Table 4. Fits/Forecasts

Appendix B. Tutorial on the R Statistical Language

The R statistical language can be freely downloaded via the following web-site: www.r-project.org. There is an option to select your operating system, a location from which to download, and so on. From there, you simply follow the installation instructions and R should open properly.

There are many ways to use R, but here, we will keep it as simple as possible. An Excel spreadsheet can be used to prepare the data. It is important that Excel only contain the raw data – "scratch-pad" types of calculations should be omitted. The "clean" spreadsheet should be saved in the *.csv format. For this tutorial, we will use the exam scores data set ("ExamScores.csv").

When in R, choose the "File|Change dir..." option, and select the folder which contains the data you wish to analyze. Once done, enter the following command:

```
>A = read.csv("ExamScores.csv")
```

It should be noted that the ">" character is a prompt – it tells us that R is ready for a command. For this tutorial, "A" is the name of the data set. After opening the data set, we can examine its structure, via the following command:

```
>str(A)
```

This command reports the structure of the data set, and returns the following:

```
'data.frame':   1000 obs. of  2 variables:
 $ Exam1: int  84 69 86 82 79 81 81 80 80 79 ...
 $ Exam2: int  74 66 92 79 77 72 83 77 71 77 ...
```

This command tells us that we have two integer variables named "Exam1" and "Exam2," and a total of 1,000 observations. R also reports the first several values of each variable.

Now that the data set has been imported, we can ask for descriptive statistics. For this, we use the following function:

```
>summary(A)
```

The "summary" function returns the following:

```
    Exam1               Exam2
Min.    :67.00    Min.    :58.00
1st Qu.:77.00     1st Qu.:72.00
Median :80.00     Median :77.00
Mean    :79.91    Mean    :76.84
3rd Qu.:83.00     3rd Qu.:81.00
Max.    :92.00    Max.    :99.00
```

R also provides us the ability to access specific variables. In order to do this, we first refer to the data set ("A" in our case), then use "$" as a delimiter, then we use the specific variable name we wish to access. Given that the summary function doesn't provide us with the standard deviation, we will ask R to return the standard deviation for each variable, which returns the following:

```
> sd(A$Exam1)
[1] 4.127582
> sd(A$Exam2)
[1] 6.759043
```

R also has an extensive graphics library. For example, we can have R generate a histogram of one of our variables. For example, we can generate a histogram for Exam1 via the following command:

```
> hist(A$Exam1,main="Exam 1 Histogram", xlab = "Exam 1")
```

The "hist" function asks R to make a histogram from the "A" data set using the Exam1 variable. It also asks for the histogram to be titled "Exam 1 Histogram," and asks for the x-axis label to be called "Exam 1." This function provides the following output:

Exam 1 Histogram

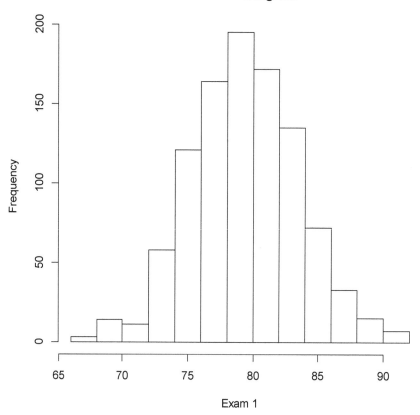

It should be noted that R also permits us to control the boundaries and widths of the outcomes in our histogram, but the details of this are left to the interested reader.

We can also use R to produce a box plot. For this example, we will produce a boxplot to include both exam scores. To accomplish this task, we will use the following command:

```
> boxplot(A$Exam1, A$Exam2, main="Box Plot", horizontal=TRUE,
        names=c("Exam 1", "Exam 2"), xlab="Score")
```

Here, we ask for each variable to be included in the box plot. Then we give the box plot a title via the "main" argument. We then ask for each box plot to have a "horizontal" orientation. We then ask each box plot to be specifically named via the "name" command. Finally, we wish to label the horizontal axis via the "xlab" command. The result of this command is as follows:

Box Plot

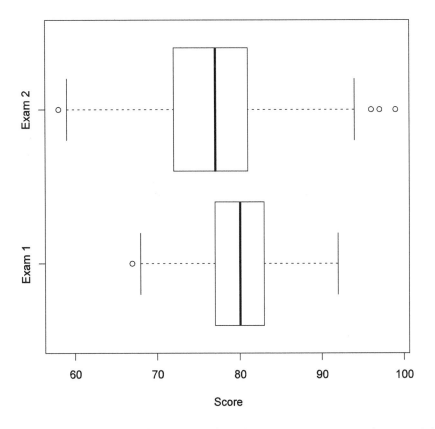

Another application of R is to perform linear regression. In this tutorial, we will explore the relationship between the Exam 1 and Exam 2 scores. To accomplish this, we use the linear model ("lm") function in R, and state that Exam 2 is the response variable, while Exam 1 is the predictor variable. This model uses data set "A." The R command for this is as follows:

```
> summary(lm(Exam2 ~ Exam1, data=A))
```

The following output is the result, telling us that the two variables are in fact related, with an R^2 value of 0.3994.

```
Call:
lm(formula = Exam2 ~ Exam1, data = A)

Residuals:
    Min      1Q   Median      3Q     Max
-17.9381 -3.7987  -0.0253  3.8528 18.1316

Coefficients:
            Estimate Std. Error t value Pr(>|t|)
(Intercept) -5.84989    3.21445   -1.82   0.0691 .
Exam1        1.03485    0.04017   25.76   <2e-16 ***
---
Signif. codes:  0 '***' 0.001 '**' 0.01 '*' 0.05 '.' 0.1 ' ' 1

Residual standard error: 5.241 on 998 degrees of freedom
Multiple R-squared:  0.3994,    Adjusted R-squared:  0.3988
F-statistic: 663.6 on 1 and 998 DF,  p-value: < 2.2e-16
```

We can take this analysis one step further by producing a scatter plot of both variables, along with the fitted regression line based on the model built above. This can be done via the following two commands:

```
> plot(A$Exam2 ~ $Exam1, xlab="Exam", ylab="Exam2",
          main="Linear Regression")
> abline(lm(A$Exam2 ~ A$Exam1))
```

These commands result in the following plot:

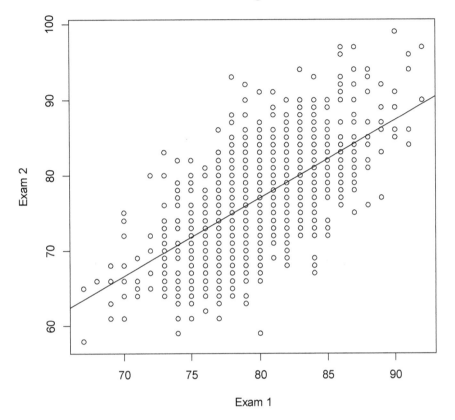

Linear Regression

This is a very brief tutorial so that you can get started using the R software. It takes a little while to get started, but with some practice, performing data analysis via R becomes second nature. I have created the following web-site that might serve as an additional R resource: www.joydivisionman.com/R.

References

Having never written a book before, I'm not exactly sure how to cite references. My knowledge of statistics has accumulated over the years to the point where most all of what has been written here came from my teaching experience. As such, the references I cite below are from books that I like, books I have used in the past, or books in my collection that history has deemed as important.

Albright, C., Winston, W. and Zappe, C. "Data Analysis and Decision Making, 4th Edition." Cengage Learning. Cincinnati, OH. 2011.

Bowerman, B., O'Connell, R. and Murphee, E. "Business Statistics in Practice." Irwin/McGraw-Hill. New York, New York. 2011.

Brightman, H. "Statistics in Plain English." Southwestern Publishing. Cincinnati, OH. 1986.

Cox, D.R. "The Regression Analysis of Binary Sequences (with Discussion)." Journal of the Royal Statistical Society. Vol. 20, pp 215-242.

Gaither, N. and Frazier, G. "Operations Management." Southwestern Publishing. Cincinnati, OH. 2002.

Hosmer, D.W. and Lemeshow,S. "Applied Logistic Regression." Wiley Interscience. New York, NY. 2000.

Sharpe, N., DeVeaux, R. and Velleman, P. "Business Statistics: A First Course." Pearson Higher Education. New York, New York. 2014.

Sternstein, M. "Statistics." Barron's College Review Series. Hauppauge, New York. 1996.

Wonnacott, T.H. and Wonnatott, R.J. "Introductory Statistics." John Wiley & Sons. New York, New York. 1990.